Praise for A Question of Heritage: An Adoption Story

This book by Judith Pachino is a page-turning personal account where hearts are sometimes broken, but the human spirit perseveres. Pachino takes us to a societal time, touching on issues that the world veiled. Pre-marital relations, unwanted pregnancies, homes for pregnant girls, were cloaked in a black box of secrecy. Pachino's descriptive words turn that world inside out as she introduces deep, emotional feelings, and difficult actions that had to be made to conform to the times. The author, through flawless transition, takes the reader to the other side as well, writing with knowledgeable candor of how an adopted child might look at the world, and feel love perhaps differently, sometimes distantly.

This book reads itself to you. It's the kind of book that should come with the warning: "You won't be able to put this book down once you start reading." Pachino's story is something to which many can relate. The reader will feel the heart-wrenching stress of its characters, and it will make readers feel by book's end that these are people we know or have known. For that alone, we are better off by Pachino's shared insight. For those who have lived the lives chronicled by Pachino, this is a must read. For those who need to learn of these sensitivities, it is a great read, a teaching read.

- Phil Jacobs, award winning editor and journalist

A Question of Heritage
An Adoption Story

by
Judith Jo Pachino

Publisher's Note

This is a book of fiction based on the author's life story. When possible, it is a recollection of events related to the best of the author's knowledge. All identities have been changed or are a composite. Places and incidents are either a product of the author's imagination or used fictitiously.

Acknowledgments

Thank you to professional writers Bracha Goetz, Jim Williams and Phil Jacobs for their encouragement, expertise, and valuable advice.

Thank you to Stan Lebovic for his friendship, guidance and the perfect cover design.

Thank you to my family and friends for their encouragement, love and support as I traveled the challenging road to discovery.

For all those touched by an adoption

Prologue

October 2007

Noah arrived home after a thirteen hour workday, the newest scheduling idiocy, an 8am to 9pm shift at the pharmacy. He hung up his coat on the banister thinking that he really should use the closet but too tired to make the effort. The house was unusually dark and silent. Where is Ellen? He thought as he quietly made his way up the stairs and peeked into their bedroom. With just the glow from the adjacent bathroom to light the space, he found his wife of nineteen years cocooned under a mound of blankets, a cold compress covering her eyes.

"Ellen, are you sick?" he whispered as he padded softly into the room.

"Hi Noah," Ellen replied, removing the compress and stretching out to her full 5'2" length. Abruptly she exclaimed, "I had the most awful day – you can't imagine!" They both grimaced from the intensity of her voice as she threw off the covers and swiveled to sit on the edge of the bed.

Noah sat down beside her. Turning, he looked deeply into her troubled, chocolate brown, hazel specked eyes and asked, "What happened?"

"You must be hungry. I'll come down with you and we can get you some dinner. I have spaghetti warming in the oven and soup on the stove."

"Don't worry about that right now," he said with worried impatience. "Tell me what happened."

"Finding proof that I'm Jewish is going to be even harder than I thought – virtually impossible!" Ellen burst out. "First, I spoke to Rabbi Golden and he thinks we may need to do a conversion of doubt with three male witnesses watching our daughters dunk naked in the mikvah (spiritual bath). Then, Rachel called and remains insistent that this be resolved as soon as possible no matter what I or we have to do. Finally, to compound the issue a hundred-fold, Mrs. Kaplan from the Jewish Adoption Center called and told me she lost my file! Kaput! Not there! My whole family history gone!" Ellen unloaded breathlessly.

"Wait a minute. Slow down! One thing at a time."

"My thoughts exactly. Okay," she said taking a deep breath. "Let's start from the beginning."

Chapter One

April 1962

With a determined gait, the Coleman College sophomore, a pretty brunette 5'4" tall, slightly plump, pink tinged complexion, big brown eyes and a warm, welcoming smile walked across the Baltimore County campus. The sun hung low in the sky as Jo cut through the path between two buildings carefully sidestepping a blooming rose bush. The heady scent of roses stayed with her as she entered Lorry Hall with just a few minutes to spare before her evening class.

Jo met her friend Peggy just outside their classroom. They both reached for the knob at the same time. Giggling, Peggy pulled the door open and ushered Jo in. "Hi Jo," she said brushing her straight blond bangs out of her eyes, "ready for another scintillating evening of English Lit?"

"Of course. It's the highlight of my day," Jo replied, laughing.

The two moved into the small classroom and took their seats behind the long desks.

"Steve and I drove to Washington, D.C. last Sunday. He took me to a far out coffeehouse just off the mall. Did you know that Philip Roth is going to speak on a panel with Ralph Ellison next month?" she said excitedly.

"No," said Jo. "That's interesting."

"I think so too," Peggy continued. "Anyway, on the way back to the car we went to the mall to see the cherry blossom trees," she said, leaning close to Jo. "They were intoxicating just like Steve's kisses."

"Oooo. That sounds so romantic," Jo responded.

"It was. We held hands the whole time, and he bought me a long-stemmed rose from a flower stand we passed on the way back to the car."

"I think he's a keeper," Jo replied, looking intently at Mr. Feldman, their professor, as he entered and took his position at the front of the room.

A few hours later, the girls emerged from the building. Jo shivered in the cool air and pulled her favorite pink cardigan more tightly around her. Waving goodbye to Peggy, she headed for her car parked on a nearby street. Jo looked up into a pair of charming hazel eyes that crinkled in the corners as Lenny smiled and fell into step beside her. Lenny, her English Literature professor, with his crew cut, medium build adorned with a stylish two button gray suit and a smart white shirt and black wingtips, looked successful and self-assured. Jo's heart did flip-flops as she gazed at him even though she had just spent the past two hours staring at him while trying to concentrate on his lecture. He is so handsome, she thought.

"Did you enjoy tonight's class?" he asked.

"I was riveted," she answered. "How have you been?"

"Better, now that I see you."

"Such a sweet talker – you are."

"It's true. I've been waiting to see you all day."

Reaching Jo's car, Lenny asked, "Shall we head to our diner?"

"Sure. I'm rather hungry."

Checking around quickly for onlookers and finding none, Lenny opened Jo's car door for her with gentlemanly good manners. "I'll follow you," he said.

"Good plan professor."

Lenny pulled into the parking space next to Jo's at the diner. Sliding into the passenger side of Jo's car, he leaned over and gave her a satisfying, passionate kiss. Jo sighed deeply as she lost herself in Lenny's embrace. They had been dating just a few short months, but she was hooked.

As they walked toward the entrance hand in hand, Jo decided that the diner they frequented was quaint in its own unique way. The food truly was good and plentiful and the clientele friendly enough although much older than Jo or Lenny.

"I do like this restaurant, Lenny, but couldn't we try one closer to the campus next time?" Jo asked.

"Darling, I know it's a bit far, but I have to be discreet. I'm proud to be dating you, you know that, but as your professor I have to be careful that no one sees us together."

"Of course. I understand," Jo said feeling sophisticated.

"Besides, I love to have you all to myself," he whispered, putting his arm around her shoulders and pulling her close as they entered.

Over burgers and shakes, they talked about Jo's work and Lenny's classes. The light banter was mixed with very real sexual tension and they made quick work of the meal. As Lenny followed Jo home, they kept the mood alive by sending meaningful looks back and forth at each stop sign.

Home for Jo was a one room rental in a decent part of town conveniently located near the Baltimore college campus. She was ecstatic to have her own space for the first time in her young life. During her nineteen years, Jo had lived in too many places that she couldn't call home. After her mother died when she was seven years old, she was left with only her father to care for her. Her father owned and managed a bar. Long hours and evening work made it difficult for him to be there to watch over his small daughter. Fortunately they had a vast extended family in the area, and father and daughter lived for short stints with various family members. Moving constantly from place to place ended when Jo was ten and her father remarried. Although she had a place to live and a stable environment with her father and stepmother, her stepmother's home was ruled with an iron will and strict rules which challenged the sensitive, young woman and caused much discord in the family. Unfortunately, tragedy rapidly struck again, and her father died just after Jo's high school graduation. It became increasingly difficult for her to live with her stepmother once her father was gone, and a year later, she moved herself from the house of her stepmother to a boarding home with the kind Mrs. Levinter near her work and school.

Jo worked by day as a receptionist in a doctor's office and by night she was a college student. She fixed up her room with love and appreciation on a very limited budget and made it cozy, a place that was finally hers.

Boarding with Mrs. Levinter had its advantages as well as its challenges, but Jo found the arrangement to her liking. She enjoyed conversing and frequent shared meals with the likeable widow, and Mrs. Levinter grew to care for and worry about Jo. The two seemed in total accord except for one thing, Jo's failure to heed the house rule of no males in upstairs rooms. Having caught Jo with Lenny on more than one occasion, Mrs. Levinter warned Jo that her promiscuous behavior would not be abided.

As they ascended the stairs to her room just before ten, Jo held her fingers to her lips and whispered, "We must be very quiet so as not to disturb Mrs. Levinter."

Once inside with the door closed and locked, Lenny pulled Jo toward him and caressed her face and arms. His kisses heated things up and from there they made rapid work of undressing and fell into each other's arms laughing. Their joining was quick and explosive. Afterward, Lenny held Jo for a time, but he did not stay the night.

"Do you really have to leave so soon?" Jo motioned for him to stay.

"I have an early start tomorrow. Sorry darling," he replied as he kissed her good night.

Lenny failed to notice the troubled widow peek from her doorway as the door closed quietly behind him.

Chapter Two

In the same city just a few miles north, Sandra and Jay were getting ready for bed. They looked over at each other with tired smiles. Michael, their feisty six-year old, had woken from a bad dream and it had taken time and patience to comfort him back to sleep.

Sandra lifted her slender arms up over her head and settled her nightgown over her finely proportioned 5'6" body. Short sleek, dark brown hair and eyes, high rouged cheekbones and red lipstick-colored lips contrasted sharply with the plain modest nightgown. Her beauty nonetheless was quite visible. Jay turned and smiled. He truly appreciated his wife's assets.

Jay was a fit specimen in his own right. Years of athletic training and success had kept his big 6'2" frame toned. Although, his days were spent as a businessman in a large corporation, he still found time to exercise and enjoy all things sports. Just like Sandra, he had dark hair and eyes, but his eyes were warmer in color and his hair wavy and a bit unruly.

"Maybe we should move Michael to the room next to us," said Jay. "I think the attic leading from his closet is scaring him."

"I agree," Sandra replied, "he doesn't want me to store any of his clothes in that closet and he doesn't even like it when I open the door. I already moved all his things to the small closet on the other side of the room. Let's move him this week."

"Okay. I have time on Sunday afternoon to help you."

"Great. It's a date."

Sandra and Jay had been married for almost nine years. They lived in a small house with their son as well as Sandra's mother. Sandra's mother was widowed young and became blinded by a fluke accident. That is how she came to be living with the young family. Sandra and Jay generously provided the first floor master bedroom with the attached bathroom for Mother taking the largest of four small bedrooms on the second floor for themselves.

Settling herself in their bed that practically filled the room, Sandra turned toward Jay and said sadly, "Michael asked again today about a baby brother. His friend Larry just found out that his mother is expecting. How children don't know when their mothers keep getting bigger and bigger I can't quite understand. Anyway, Doris is due in a few weeks and I guess they felt it was time to prepare the boys."

"Sandra, please don't get upset. I know that it's hard when he asks, but just tell him that we have him and he is a very special boy and that is enough," Jay replied emphatically.

"That is not so easy to do. He keeps asking and asking and gets himself worked up with what he wants. Mother didn't know what to do today. She kept answering him and trying to reason with him. Finally she tickled him silly, and he got distracted."

"He'll grow out of it. Michael's birth was difficult, and the doctors have all agreed that your tubes are blocked and there is no more than can be done. We have to be thankful for Michael. Simply tell him that we all want things that we cannot have and leave it at that."

"I'll try. I'll tell Mother as well."

"Please don't get upset all over again. Honey, I thought we had moved past this," Jay said, pulling her close.

"Yes. Of course we have. You are right."

"Now, let's get some sleep. I love you."

"I love you too. Good night."

Chapter Three

The party was in full swing as Carol and Jo entered the door. Petite and skinny with long brown hair and green eyes, Carol was perpetual motion. Jo's best friend since grade school, it was Carol who kept Jo up to date with the latest goings on in music, movies, fashion and gossip.

As they approached the party venue, rock music boomed down the hallway. "Bobbie sure knows how to throw a party!" Carol exclaimed happily. "By the way Jo, you look fab in that lemon dress!"

The small apartment was filled with college-aged kids doing the twist. Benny and Ross, two of their friends, grabbed them by the hands. In a blink, Jo and Carol were on the dance floor twisting away.

About a half hour later, Jo motioned to Ross that she needed a drink. They wandered over to the refreshment table.

"It's so good to see you, Jo," Ross said.

"It's nice to see you too."

"How are your classes going? "I haven't seen you in ages."

"I know. I know. School and work are both great. It's neat living on my own, but I'm really busy."

"Do you have any time for dating, Jo?" Ross asked hope written all over his boyish face.

Before she could answer, Randall, William, and Marty joined them peppering Jo with questions. As

Carol watched from the dance floor, she figured that Jo was completely unaware of the intense looks on the boys' faces as she innocently flirted with them. Jo was quintessentially nice and this quality drew the boys to her. Regardless, Jo was having fun, and Carol was glad she had convinced her to come to the party instead of sitting by the phone waiting for Lenny to call.

Meanwhile, Ross was trying hard to keep Jo entertained, but before he made his move and asked Jo out, Marty had grabbed Jo's hand, and she was heading back on the dance floor with him. Ross had missed his opportunity, and Carol saw him flinch.

The girls danced until their waists and hips hurt, and then laughing they left the party.

"Wasn't that a blast!" Carol screamed as they went out the door unaware of how loud she was.

"Shhhh Carol. Yes, it was a ball. I had the best time catching up with everyone."

"Ross looked very interested in you. But so did Marty and Randall and William," Carol teased.

"Oh no. Carol. They are just friends. Besides, I'm taken."

"I know that, but no one else does."

"I do wish that Lenny had come with us tonight. I would have loved to introduce him around. He would have been a hit for sure."

"I would like to meet him sometime myself."

"I know. I want him to meet you too. It's a bit annoying that we have to keep our dating a secret, but he insists that he is not ready to share me with anyone and cherishes our alone time together. Isn't that romantic?"

"Yes. I think so," Carol answered hesitantly, "but I would like to meet him soon."

"Don't worry, I will make sure you do," Jo declared.

Chapter Four

May 1962

Jo woke to clear skies and chirping birds as she opened the bedroom window and breathed in the fresh spring air. Unfortunately, the air wasn't helping. She heard the distant sound of the phone ringing downstairs in the foyer and then the hushed voice of Mrs. Levinter as she answered it. Moments later, she heard heavy footsteps on the stairs followed by soft-knuckled knocking on her door.

Mrs. Levinter announced, "Jo, the phone is for you. I am leaving to visit my sister and will be gone most of the day."

"Thank you. I'll be right down," Jo called grabbing her pink and white checked robe before opening the door.

"Hi Jo, what are you up to today?" asked Carol. "I know you have studying to do, but are you up for a matinee? *State Fair* is playing at the Senator."

"I don't think I can. I'm feeling a bit queasy. Maybe I caught some kind of bug."

"Oh. I am sorry Jo. Do you need anything?"

"No, but thank you. I think I'll rest a bit and try to do some studying later."

"OK. Ring me if you need anything."

"I will. Thanks. Have fun at the movie if you go. I heard it was good. Peggy went with Steve last week."

"Drink some tea. I'll call you later."

Jo had just made her way back up the stairs when she was overcome with nausea. Flying down the short hallway to the bathroom, she retched into the commode relieved that she had made it in time. From her crouched position, she settled back on her heels and took deep, calming breaths. Oddly, she became hungry. Shaking her head, she washed up and then headed back downstairs to Mrs. Levinter's tiny galley kitchen where she made herself some tea and toast.

Shortly after noon, the phone rang again. This time, Jo raced downstairs to answer it.

"Hello Lenny," Jo grinned as she heard his voice.

"Are you studying hard for your finals next week – especially English Lit. I hear the professor makes the exam particularly difficult," quipped Lenny.

"Ha, ha," said Jo. "Yes professor, I am studying. It wouldn't do for me to fail your class. Would it, darling?" She said coyly. "That is what I was thinking this morning when I felt ill. Luckily that passed and then I was hungry. Isn't that strange? Anyway, I should be ready for the test Monday."

"You were sick. How so?"

"I was nauseous. I thought I might have caught something. Maybe I should buy a big bottle of Listerine and kill millions of germs like the commercials say."

"That's an idea. Listerine will kill anything. Are you feeling better?"

"Yes. I feel fine now. Carol called and wanted me to go see *State Fair* with her, but I told her I couldn't. Now I wish I had gone."

"I think staying home was a good choice. Maybe you should take it easy and rest."

"I think I'll be okay today. Yesterday, I had the same thing and once it passed I was fine."

"That's puzzling," Lenny said softly.

"I think so too, but I'm fine now. I really am."

"I have to go," he said cutting the call short.

"Don't you want to come over and check on me? Just to be sure."

"I can't today. I have a lot of paperwork to do. I'll ring you later."

"Ok. Then I'll go back to my studying – ho hum. Bye, Lenny."

"Bye, Jo."

After her English Literature final the next evening, Jo walked slowly toward her car swinging her navy pocketbook back and forth from the strap in patient yet eager anticipation of an evening with Lenny. She stopped briefly beneath a pair of large maple trees to artfully adjust her white-laced blouse into the waistband of her flared mint green skirt, and that is precisely where Lenny caught up to her.

"Lenny, that was a very hard test. I thought you were kidding," she said, a big smile on her face as she turned to face him with her hands on her hips pocketbook looped through one arm and eyes huge and challenging.

"I am sure you did fine. You have been my most attentive student."

"That was easy to do professor," she said sidling closer toward him.

"Jo, how are you feeling?" He said stepping back a pace.

"Fine now."

"Not before?"

"Well, actually I did have a hard time this morning getting to work. I was queasy again, and I ended up being late for work. My boss wasn't happy."

"That's too bad. I'm really sorry to hear that," Lenny hesitated a moment and then resolutely said, "I have to go. Take care, Jo. I hope you feel better."

"What? Oh... ok. I thought we were going for some dinner."

"No. Not tonight," he said bluntly. "I better get to work on the exams. Grades are due by the end of the week."

"Okay. Will you ring me later?"

"I'll try."

Bewildered, Jo watched as Lenny abruptly turned and headed to his Chevy sedan parked down the street failing to kiss her goodbye or see her safely to her car with the gentlemanly good manners that she so loved. What was that all about? Jo wondered. Disappointed, she made her way home and fixed herself a light dinner.

The next few days were a repeat of the past few and Jo was finding the routine disconcerting. Each morning she battled nausea, and her late arrivals at work were duly noted. With her final exam on Wednesday looming, she had no time to think about it. Blaming the weird illness on her hectic week, she concentrated on making it to her last exam on Wednesday. To keep her flagging spirits up, she spent long moments imagining the upcoming weekend and the celebratory dinner date at an upscale D.C. restaurant Lenny promised her to mark the end of her college semester.

As she handed in her Intro to Sociology final, she breathed a sigh of relief. Jo smiled at her professor and then headed to her car hoping that Lenny would be waiting. He was not there. She leaned on the hood of the light blue Buick Century she inherited from her father for a few minutes and then decided to wait inside the car. She turned on the radio and half-listened as the music of the Everly Brothers, Connie Francis, Brenda Lee and Elvis Presley played. Her anxiety grew. Thirty minutes went by, but Lenny still did not appear. Deflated, Jo drove slowly home wondering what had happened to Lenny.

Once home safely, Jo rang Carol.

"Hey Jo, how was the Sociology final?" asked Carol.

"It was pretty easy. Professor Stein wrote a fair exam. I found the material easy to understand, and I like the subject. Carol, I'm worried. Lenny is acting strangely."

"In what way?" Carol inquired as she moved the phone closer to her ear.

"He met me on the way to my car Monday, but then didn't ask me to have dinner and ran off without even checking that I was in my car. Today, he didn't show up at all. He hasn't called. I hope we're still on for Saturday night."

"What did he say to you?"

"That's the thing. He didn't say much at all. I keep going over it in my mind and I don't know."

"What did you say to him on Monday?"

"I told him the exam was hard and made a comment about Listerine being good for germs – oh that was after I told him that I had been ill again Monday morning and ended up late for work."

"Jo, I spoke to you Tuesday, and you said that you were late to work then. Were you sick this morning again?"

"Yesssss...," Jo said slowly suddenly miles away, the long, green phone cord trailing behind her as she paced back and forth through the foyer and out toward the kitchen.

Jo was thinking about the snow. There had been a huge snowstorm, a Noreaster they called it, that blanketed the eastern United States just last month. Over ten inches of snow had fallen on Baltimore and the city had been paralyzed. Electricity lines were down and it had been a rough few days. But for Jo, it had been a magical time. Lenny had followed her home just as the snow was getting strong. She had invited him in for the first time. Luckily, Mrs. Levinter had called just before the electricity had gone out and informed Jo that she would be staying at her sister's. Jo happily realized the house was theirs for the night. As they sipped tea and discussed little things, the lights had gone out not only in her apartment but the entire neighborhood. Pitch blackness was all they saw when they looked out her window. It didn't seem safe for Lenny to drive home and so a turning point in their relationship had presented itself. They came together laughing about fate and life and love. As the apartment cooled down, they heated up, and she gave herself to him for the first time. Listening to the snow falling while lying in Lenny's arms and feeling his heart beat strongly beneath her ear had been heavenly.

Her meandering thoughts traveled back a little farther in time settling on her second week of the semester. Jo saw herself sitting off to the side in the front row of seats paying rapt attention to her professor, Mr. Feldman, as he was enthusiastically discussing Hemingway's stylistic approach and vivid, brutal descriptions of bull fights in his masterpiece, *The Sun Also Rises*. Mr. Feldman caught her eye many times and she felt that he was showering her with attention. She knew she was just fantasizing, but it was fun nonetheless. Later, after class was over, Mr. Feldman had stopped her on the way out and told her he would like to discuss her work and could he walk her to her car. Beyond flattered, Jo readily consented. During the all too brief walk, during which they didn't talk about her course work at all, Mr. Feldman introduced himself as Lenny and pleasantly entertained Jo with a few humorous anecdotes about college life when he was an undergrad. Jo found him incredibly handsome and interesting. When they reached the car, he asked if he could take her out for a light dinner the following week. Happily surprised, she accepted. He lightly touched her hand as he said goodbye and walked away. Jo had smiled from ear to ear the whole way home and had called Carol right away to tell her of the wonderful thing that had just happened.

Lenny, Jo thought as her knees gave way and she dropped to a seat on the floor.

Forced back to the present by insistent sounds coming from the phone still clasped to her ear, she realized someone was shouting at her. It was Carol. Jo grappled to make out the words, "Jo, are you okay? Are you still there? What happened?"

"Carol," Jo shrank down even farther on the floor, holding the phone in a death grip and covered the mouthpiece tightly with her mouth as she whispered, "I think I may be in trouble."

Carol was stunned but ever the Girl Scout, she rose to the occasion. "Jo, I'm on my way. Pack an overnight bag. You will stay with Mom and me tonight," she stated.

"I don't know. I need to think. Oh my goodness. What am I going to do? Do you think Lenny will marry me? What am I going to do!" Jo exclaimed loudly. Holding her hand over her mouth to quiet herself, she realized with intense relief that Mrs. Levinter was out for the evening and had not heard her outcry.

"I'm coming over to get you. Pack a bag. I'll be there in fifteen minutes."

"Thanks Carol," Jo stammered out, "you are a true friend. I'll be ready."

Carol lived with her widowed mother, so as Carol gently knocked on her mother's bedroom door, explained that Jo needed to stay over, borrowed the keys to the car and raced to Jo's apartment, Jo wandered around the room aimlessly. She tried to focus on putting some items together, but simply could not do it. Fifteen minutes later, she had managed to get a bag out of the closet and fall on the bed beside it. Tears began to flow unchecked down her cheeks, but she didn't notice. She was jarred from her trance when Carol's knock reverberated through the house.

Jo slowly trudged to the front door and opened it. Carol was truly spooked, but she led Jo back upstairs to her room and pushed her into the closest chair. Carol ran around the bedroom gathering toiletries and sleepwear and some extra underwear.

She couldn't wait to get Jo to her house where her mother could help. At nineteen, this was way out of her league of experience.

"Come on, Jo," Carol insisted. "Let's get going now." Jo just nodded and let Carol pull her and her overnight bag along.

Fifteen long minutes later for Carol, they arrived at the Rosen home without incident, although Carol was still nervous that Jo was going to freak. Carol pushed Jo into her bedroom and motioned for her to lie down on the bed.

"How are you feeling, Jo?"

"Kind of numb. Do you think I should call Lenny? I just realized that I don't even have his phone number. He always called me. I thought it was so gentlemanly, but now I don't know," she said, shaking her head. "He was punctual and we made plans when we were together for the next date, so I never really needed to call him. Now, I need his number and I don't have it," she rambled.

"Don't worry, Jo. We'll look it up in the phone book. I'm sure he meant to give it to you."

"Do you really think so? I guess you're right," Jo answered her own question. "I'm just frightened. What if he isn't ready to be a father and husband? What if he doesn't want me?" Jo wondered out loud as she started to cry.

For the first time, Jo realized how odd the relationship with Lenny had been and how little she truly knew about him. She found him exceedingly handsome. She loved his take charge attitude and his smooth and stylish ways. She loved the ideas and literature that he had made come alive for her. In contrast to the boys her age who seemed and were so young, the fact that he was much older and more mature was incredibly appealing. All in all, dating Lenny had made her feel sophisticated.

The freedom she had felt this semester as she worked and studied and lived on her own had been heady for her after all the years trying to please everyone and being dependent. Her stepmother's mother, Bea, had been the worst with her constant picking on every little thing Jo did, and Jo could never make good in her cruel eyes. Although kind and loving, her stepmother had an endless list of rules. Deeply, Jo had missed her own mother and her father as well. Her father had worked every evening at the tavern he owned and although often a missing presence, she had loved him and longed for him. As she sat thinking, the tears continued to course down her cheeks. Jo began to feel the intense despair that had plagued her throughout her high school years. What a mess she had made of her newfound freedom.

She should have been more wary, she thought. Lenny had convinced her that sleeping together was what mature, sophisticated adults did. Lenny had used condoms. He had told her not to worry about pregnancy, because he was taking precautions. She remembered the conversation clearly, but now she felt that he had pressured her and she had given in too quickly and easily. At times like that day and especially today, Jo missed her mother so much her heart felt like it was breaking. She would talk to Mrs. Rosen, Carol's mother. The Rosen family had been wonderful to Jo since Carol and Jo had become friends in fifth grade when Jo's father had remarried and they had moved in a few blocks down the street. Mrs. Rosen would help Jo figure out what to do.

Sitting next to Jo holding her hand and carefully watching Jo's face for a clue how to proceed, Carol's thoughts swirled with images from their childhood sleepovers usually in this very room. As little girls they had played dress up sneaking into Carol's mother's room to borrow her scarves and shoes, hats and pocketbooks. They had spent hours and hours playing with Carol's Barbie dolls and she remembered their disappointment with the many ruined attempts at sewing Barbie clothes themselves. She recalled sitting and laughing as they learned how to paint their toes with nail polish, and the mess they had made on her new sheets. Fondly, she thought of the hundreds of nights they had curled up in the twin beds which they had pushed together so that they could lay only inches away face to face as they talked about everything imaginable. They shared every secret. While covered to their necks with the blue and white floral bedspreads, they discussed the silly and then mean girls at school and later it was boys, so many discussions about boys. How they looked and smelled and talked and walked and were incredibly confusing. They were still terribly confusing, Carol thought as she worried over Jo's likely predicament.

Jolting Carol from her reverie, Jo hesitantly asked, "Do you think your mother is still up? Do you think she could help me?"

"I'm sure she's up. I'll go get her right away. Everything will be fine, Jo, you'll see. I'll be right back with Mom," Carol responded without hesitation, relieved to pass the baton to her mother.

Mrs. Rosen rushed from her bedroom at Carol's insistence that something was wrong. Still wrapping her full length turquoise night robe around her, she entered Carol's bedroom and swiftly moved toward Jo. "Oh my, what has happened to you?" she asked immediately. Enfolding Jo in her ample embrace, she dabbed at Jo's new flow of tears with the tip of her robe with one hand and rubbed up and down Jo's trembling back with the other. Patiently, Mrs. Rosen waited until Jo calmed enough to speak.

Choking on her words but needing to get them out quickly, Jo explained her relationship with Lenny and the path it has taken. Finally, in a voice barely above a whisper, she got to the crux of the problem. "I've been nauseous each morning for at least a week. I think I may be pregnant."

Chapter Five

Mrs. Rosen gently prodded her for specifics.

"Are you sure you're pregnant? Have you confirmed this with a doctor?"

Jo shook her head no.

"Have you missed your period?"

Jo shrugged her shoulders. "I have a strange cycle. I think—it should have come already." Helplessly, she shrugged again.

"Have you spoken to the boy that is responsible for this?"

"No, I haven't called him yet. Do you think I should or do you think …" she trailed off. "Should I see the doctor first?"

"Let me see," Mrs. Rosen paused and considered. "Jo, tomorrow, we will make an appointment for you to see a doctor, and I will go with you to the appointment if you would like. That is the first thing. As far as your young man, I can't say. I assume he will do the right thing and marry you if you are pregnant."

Jo was fine with the appointment and relieved that Mrs. Rosen was willing to take her, since she was unsure of herself and fearful to go alone. As for Lenny, she felt fairly confident that he would do the right thing by her, although quietly she admitted, "I don't know. We haven't known each other very long and we haven't talked about any future or marriage."

"That is quite unfortunate," Mrs. Rosen said sadly as she shook her head.

Feeling the quiet rebuke and turning crimson, Jo lowered her head. She felt her own mother looking down on her and shaking her head too. "I'm so sorry," Jo muttered unable to look into Mrs. Rosen's face. How could she have let things get so out of control? she asked herself.

As understanding dawned, Mrs. Rosen sighed sadly. She had first hand knowledge and experience with the difficulties of parenting alone. Widowed at the age of 32 with an eight year old daughter, Jeanette Rosen had struggled. Through the years, she had been pitied and bullied and discounted. With fortitude, she had managed to eke out a modest living as a teller in a bank and she was grateful for the work, but it was family money that had allowed Jeanette and her young daughter the cushion to manage in a world where women were underpaid in the workplace compared to their male counterparts even when they were the sole breadwinner in the family. The simple fact was that most women needed husbands to succeed in this world, and she was profoundly sad that her young friend, who had already suffered great tragedy and loss, may be forced to face harsh realities without a husband.

Mrs. Rosen gently lifted Jo's chin with her forefinger and looked deeply into her eyes. "Carol and I will help you through this and all will be okay. Let's check with the doctor first and take it from there. I'll make the appointment first thing tomorrow. For now, we must all try to get some sleep."

"Thank you for everything, Mrs. Rosen," Jo blinked back more tears as she watched Mrs. Rosen and Carol walk out of the bedroom. She heard them talking in hushed tones. Too weary to undress, Jo climbed into the bed and was asleep by the time Carol reentered the room a few minutes later.

Jo woke exhausted from a restless sleep. The mirror reflected red swollen eyes and a worried expression that matched Jo's external appearance with her inner turmoil. Battling nausea and nervousness, Jo called in sick to work. Mrs. Rosen had followed through and made an appointment with Dr. Goodman's office. Luckily, they had a cancellation late that very day. With the appointment looming and Carol busy studying for a final, Jo rested in bed consumed with thoughts of Lenny. Jo was naturally an optimist; she proceeded through life with a smile on her face and belief that good was waiting just around the corner. Putting her worries aside, she hoped with all her heart that Lenny would stand by her if need be. She imagined that he would be surprised by the news, but unquestionably supportive, professing his undying love and insisting they marry right away. His impromptu proposal would be on one knee with outstretched arms, and she would she tearfully respond "yes". Continuing her fantasy, she envisioned in detail the amazing life they would make together and the beautiful baby that would fill their new pink nursery. A smile on her lips, she imagined a little girl with Lenny's hazel eyes looking up and smiling at her adoring parents with big, rosy cheeks. They would live near the college and Jo would be able to stay home with their daughter plus attend classes when Lenny wasn't teaching. Their love would be apparent to all who saw them. Jo sighed happily.

Carol popped her head in the room. "Hey Jo. I think I'm finished studying for a while. I should be ready for my final tomorrow. How're you feeling? Any better?"

"Yes," Jo smiled broadly still lost in her reverie. Then she noted that she was indeed feeling less nauseous and actually hungry. "Would it be okay to make some toast or something? I'm hungry."

"Great. Come on. Maybe we'll have some time to go shopping if we leave early for the doctor's appointment."

"That sounds good to me."

"We can stop by the record store and see if they have the *West Side Story* soundtrack. Every time I go in, it's sold out. We could listen to it later. Wasn't Tony dreamy?" Carol said in a singsong voice dancing around the floor as if she was Maria dancing with Tony.

"Yes, he was," Jo agreed as she pictured Lenny's face. He was the one that was dreamy, she mused. Jo had decided that she would call him later that day if he didn't call her first. She was pretty sure that he would call, because he would want to confirm for Saturday night, and she planned to tell him what was happening as soon as possible instead of waiting until she saw him in person. That seemed the right thing to do. With a plan in place, she felt hopeful.

The girls ate their breakfast and then spent the early afternoon shopping for the latest clothing styles. They loved the bright pastels that seemed to be all the rage. They hit the record store before they made their way to the doctor's office, and Carol was thrilled that the *West Side Story* album was there for her to buy. Jo smiled at the simple thing that had made her friend dance around in circles. Outside the doctor's office, they waited for Mrs. Rosen who came directly from her job at the bank. They decided that Carol should get a soda down the block at the corner drugstore for propriety sake, while Jo and Mrs. Rosen made their way inside.

The office had strict rules and only Jo was allowed back in the examining room, so Mrs. Rosen waited in the waiting area. With knocking knees and pumping heart, Jo followed the nurse down the hall. The disapproving nurse, who seemed to know just why this young unmarried woman was seeking the good doctor's counsel, prattled on about young women and their loose morals. Jo was mortified. She waited what felt like an eternity until the doctor entered the room. He was short, stocky, and Jo found him both doctor and fatherly-looking with very kind eyes. Once she had stammered out that she believed she may be pregnant, he took her hand in both of his.

"Let's take one step at a time, why don't we miss." As he paused, he smiled at Jo and continued, "I need you to take this glass jar and urinate in it. Hold it steady beneath you as you pee. Halfway will be enough. The bathroom is right down the hall. Now, go ahead and bring it back to this room when you are finished. I will return shortly."

It took Jo full minutes with shaking hands to accomplish her goal, but finally she had done as the doctor instructed.

"Good work, Miss Engle. I will send this off to be tested. It will take two weeks to get the results, but I will call the number you wrote on your paperwork as soon as I have the news for you. Do you have any questions?"

Jo had many questions, but none that she felt she could ask that day. "No, Dr. Goodman. Thank you."

Mrs. Rosen rose as she entered the waiting room. Both women made their way to the door. "Thank you Mrs. Rosen. Dr. Goodman was very kind to me. He said he will call in two weeks. However will I wait that long?"

"You will do what must be done, Jo." Those words reverberated in Jo's mind. Yes, I must, she thought.

Throughout the day, Jo had imagined her conversation with Lenny. Her earlier fantasy had given her confidence that he would stand by her. She had gone through the whole scenario over and over and mentally practiced a little speech. Surely she would hear from him by dinnertime, but as day turned into evening and then night, her bravado faltered and she grew apprehensive.

Jo waited until 9 pm that evening and finally called Lenny eager to hear his voice. Earlier she and Carol had looked up Lenny's phone number in the phone book, relieved when they found it easily. Jo had convinced herself that it was simply an oversight that he had not furnished it for her previously.

With excitement, she dialed the HU4-1123 number and the phone began to ring. One ring, two, then three and finally it was picked up.

"Hello," said a female voice.

"Uh… Hello. May I speak to Lenny Feldman, please?" Jo asked brightly even though she was quite unnerved by the voice of a female answering the line.

"Who is this?"

"My name is Jo Engle. Is Lenny there?"

"Well Jo Engle, what is it that you need with my husband after 9pm at night?"

Stunned, Jo tried again. Something must have been amiss. "Do I have the correct number? Is this the residence of the Lenny Feldman that teaches at Coleman College?"

"Yes. That is my husband. Are you one of his students? If so, what do you need to speak to him about at this time of night and after the semester?"

Horrified, Jo slowly lowered the phone to its cradle. She sank to the floor with her head pounding NO, NO, NO over and over. How could this be? How could she have been so naïve, so trusting, so stupid?

She had decided to call Lenny from her own apartment instead of Carol's house. Miserably, she regretted that decision along with so many others. Alone and trembling, she sat on the floor with her knees pulled up to her chest in an upright fetal position rocking back and forth for over an hour. It was unreal. Lenny – married! She wanted to call Carol, she needed to call Carol but she couldn't bother her friend. Jo remembered that she had a final in the morning. Tomorrow she would call Carol.

Hundreds of regrets later, after she has gone over every moment of her time with the deceitful Lenny, she vowed to herself that she would manage somehow. Fantasies shattered, exhausted, she fell asleep curled on the floor embracing her belly.

Chapter Six

For the next two weeks, Jo barely functioned. Work, morning sickness and constant anxiety made an exhausting combination. She was thankful that the school semester was over and she didn't have coursework to contend with as well. The days had moved like a watched clock, which is what she had done, watched the clock, the seconds ticking with excruciating slowness. During her lunch break, she found a moment of privacy and called Dr. Goodman's office to see if the results were available. She was told that yes they were, and that the doctor's routine included time spent at the end of each day returning calls and to expect his call toward the close of business hours. Jo managed through her own endless work day, and then she rushed home.

Waiting for the call and finally having the phone ring were two different things. Taking a deep breath and carefully lifting the receiver, Jo answered.

"Miss Engle? This is Dr. Goodman."

"Yes doctor. Well…..?"

"Miss Engle, you are indeed pregnant. I hope this is happy news for you."

With her fears confirmed and her future unraveled, Jo was anything but happy. "I… don't know what I should do. I thought he would be there for me, but I found out he is married. What am I going to do?" she blurted out before she could stop herself.

33

"Oh, my dear I am so sorry to hear that." Pausing thoughtfully, he continued, "Would you like me to give you some advice?"

"Yes, doctor, please… I don't know what to do."

"Do you have anyone to help you raise your child?"

"No, I don't think so."

"In that case Miss Engle, my advice to you is to consider putting your baby up for adoption. It is your best and probably only real option. The baby will have a home with both a mother and a father and you will be free to marry and have future children with your husband. There is a wonderful agency, the Jewish Adoption Center right in town that handles adoptions. I have referred other young ladies, and it has worked out well. Would you like the phone number?"

Jo hesitated and the doctor thought she may be hoping for another option therefore he continued, "I know that many young women think about abortion, but I caution you not to do it." He persisted more forcefully and Jo could tell by his voice that he had said this many times before. "Abortion is dangerous and illegal. Please listen to me. It is very dangerous and often deadly." Noting that Jo remained silent he persisted, "Miss Engle, What do you think? Shall I give you the phone number for the adoption center?"

"Thank you doctor. Yes. You are very kind. Please hold on while I find pen and paper to write it down."

Over the following few weeks, Jo went to the library and researched articles on abortion. She found out that abortion had become a crime in the United

States in the mid-1800s. Although a criminal act, the number of illegal abortions per year in the United States alone was staggering. Woman of all races, ethnicities and religions faced the dangers of unsafe operations determining it their only choice and often paying with their very lives She read in the newspaper about a highly popular children's show host that chose to have an abortion, because she had been given a drug to help with morning sickness and found that the drug caused severe birth defects. She was scheduled to have an abortion and her doctor agreed to do the operation but the story got out and the county attorney's office planned to make a citizen's arrest and arrest both the hospital and the woman. The woman finally managed to travel to Sweden where abortion was legal, but the woman was ostracized by the public for her decision. The controversial story dominated the news for many days and made a great impression on Jo who came to the conclusion that abortion was extremely dangerous and scary as well as tremendously expensive. The woman in the news had the means to travel to Sweden but Jo did not. More importantly, Jo did not want to kill the life within her. She had not taken any dangerous drugs nor did she want to take any unnecessary risks with her health or the health of the baby. Drying her tears and then hugging her belly, she vowed to protect the life she carried.

A few days after Jo resolved to proceed with the pregnancy, she was called into Dr. Brian, her boss's office. Jo truly enjoyed her job. Her responsibilities included filing and answering the phones, and she found the work fulfilling. The women in the office were easy to work with, and the doctor had always been fair.

Her palms were sweating and her heart thumping wildly as she followed Dr. Brian into the room.

"Miss Engle," Dr. Brian began. "You have been a very fastidious worker. You are careful and courteous and the patients love your warm smile and nice disposition."

"Thank you, that is very kind."

"All true. But unfortunately, it has come to my attention that you have not been feeling very well lately. Is that so?"

"Well ... I have been a bit nauseous early in the mornings, but I have managed to be on time almost every day. I'm really trying."

"Yes. I am sure you are. But why are you nauseous so often?"

"Dr. Brian," she stammered, "I unexpectedly find myself in a rather awkward position."

"Yes, Miss Engle. Go on."

"You see.... I am ... I'm.... I'm pregnant."

Unfazed by the news he had already surmised, Dr Brian stated, "That it difficult news for me. I am glad that you have been honest with me today, but unfortunately I can no longer employ you in your present condition. The whole staff wishes you the very best."

"Dr. Brian, I feel much better, and I am able to do my work. Why must you fire me?"

"Miss Engle, we must maintain our high standards of decorum. Our patients require it, and it is our policy. It is not personal."

"What is your policy? What have I done wrong?"

"It is unfitting for this place of business to have unwed pregnant women working here. It is not proper. I am sorry to put things in such a blunt manner, but that is our policy."

"But, I really need this job. I won't be able to afford my apartment without it," she pleaded.

"I am truly sorry, but there really is nothing that can be done. I will be very glad to send you a good reference. That is all," he said dismissing her.

Jo pulled herself together enough to thank the doctor. Glumly, she said goodbye to her office "friends". Compounding her distress, it was apparent by their demeanor that they had guessed and even discussed her situation. Suffering the harsh stares of the others, her closest co-worker came forward to hug her and wish her the best. Jo was grateful beyond words for the kindness.

It was a miserable day for Jo. The weather seemed to agree, because April 1962 in Baltimore was an unusually but seasonally rainy month and that particular day the rain was sheeting down. Having left her umbrella in the office and not willing to return and retrieve it, Jo walked briskly to her car as tears and rain competed for space on her cheeks and face.

Drenched and wilted, she emerged from her car in front of Mrs. Levinter's house. She stopped short when she saw Lenny rushing toward her.

"We need to talk," he said leading her quickly away from the house and any prying eyes."

"What are you doing?" Jo asked confused. "I'm dripping wet, cold and tired, and I want to go in the house."

"Come on Jo. Let's just walk for a few minutes," he said, opening an umbrella, placing it over her head and shielding her from the rain.

"Lenny," Jo turned to him, fighting back tears, "are you married?"

"We've had some fun times, haven't we Jo?" Lenny asked, turning on the charm and smiling at her in the way that made her insides melt.

"Lenny, I called your house and a woman answered and said she was your wife."

"I didn't expect you to do that."

"Why not? I thought we were in love. Lenny," she cried, "I gave myself to you. I loved you and I thought you loved me."

"Now, now Jo. I never promised you anything."

"What do you mean, you never promised me anything? You told me you loved me and now I am pregnant, Lenny. I'm pregnant with your baby!"

"I know you are pregnant, and that is unfortunate."

"You know? How do you know? I just told you."

"I figured as much when you told me that you were nauseous. It doesn't really matter. I just came by to tell you that it's over between us. It's been fun, kid, but that is all it was – a fun time. You knew what you were getting into. Now listen to me. It's over. Don't ever contact me again for any reason. I mean it!" he said with emphasis.

"What about the baby? Don't you care about your baby?" she whispered horrified.

"It is not my baby. I took precautions," he answered snidely.

"What...what?" Jo spluttered trying to understand. How could this cold, cruel man be the same Lenny that held her in his arms, smothered her with kisses, laughed with her until they were both crying and whispered words of undying love? Grappling to form a response, Jo suddenly realized that she was alone. She turned and saw that Lenny was halfway down the block and then turning the corner. Unsheltered, exposed to the elements and the ugliness of betrayal, she watched in disbelief, but he never looked back.

Exhausted both emotionally and physically, Jo trudged back to Mrs. Levinter's and up the steps to her room wondering how the fabric of her life had unraveled so quickly. Numb, she dried herself off and changed clothes, then she went downstairs grabbing the phone like a lifeline, grateful that Mrs. Levinter was not home to overhear her broken sobs, as she called Carol.

"He really is married!" Jo hacked out between sobs. "He said the baby isn't his and he made me feel so dirty and loose. He was the one who wanted to have sex, he was the one that pushed me into it, and he was married!"

"I can't believe it!" Carol cried shocked by the news.

"He was so ruthless and heartless, and he told me to never contact him again!"

"I'm so sorry, Jo. What a cad! I can't believe he did this to you!"

"I can't understand how I thought I loved him. How could I have been so stupid?"

"You were not stupid, Jo. How could you have known? He took advantage of you. There was no way for you to know he wasn't sincere."

"I don't ever want to speak of him again. I won't ever speak of him again. Promise me you won't tell anyone about him and the way he treated me."

"Of course I won't say anything. You can count on me."

"From now on, he doesn't exist!" Jo said with finality. "No one will ever know that he is the father of my child, because he does not exist!"

Later that evening as Patsy Cline crooned "I Fall to Pieces" on the radio, Jo sentimentally looked around her wonderful, cozy apartment noting the ivory curtains that she had painstakingly sewed by hand, the mismatched end tables that she had bought from a friend that had moved, the sweet picture frames with her father and mother's images, the other assorted knickknacks that she was collecting little by little. They were tiny things that would mean nothing to anyone else, but were symbolic of freedom and independence to Jo. Unconsciously emitting a poignant sigh, she realized how fleeting it had all been. She could not keep the room. It was time to start looking for a place to live until the baby was born. She knew that it was time to call her aunt and uncle, her guardians. She needed the help of family.

Chapter Seven

For Jo, 214 Edge Road was a step back in time. The house was built circa 1920 in the colonial style with three stories and a wide front porch stretching across the entire width of the house. The dark brick exterior was broken up by white trim and shutters around the many windows fronting the house. As Jo walked up the short path to the front door, she thought back to her days spent in this house, the first of many relative homes she and her father lived in temporarily after her mother's death. Jo was unusually closely related on both her father's and mother's sides to her aunt and uncle, because her mother's sister married her father's brother. Aunt Bessie and Uncle Henry resided in 214 Edge Road and they had done so since before Jo was born. Her gaze automatically traveled to the top floor windows triggering painful memories of the numerous nights she had sat brokenhearted crying for her mother, waiting and staring out from the rightmost window. She had been so young and her mother's death so fresh. She had grappled with the brutal fact that her mother was never coming back. Her father kept explaining that her mother was dead, but Jo was incapable of understanding that concept and even if she could comprehend in a manner older than her age, she simply would not accept it. Instead, little seven-year old Jo waited and watched nightly from the window seat in her small bedroom for her mother to reappear. Over twelve years had gone by, but the pain and loss were still there just like the old house and her aunt and uncle.

As Jo knocked on the front door, she marveled at how circumstances had repeated themselves and brought her back to this exact spot once again. A father and young child came knocking years ago on the very same door, but this time she was the soon-to-be parent with a child on the way knocking for a second time on the door and hoping that the occupants would again offer their protection and the solace that was requested. Uncle Henry opened the door.

"Hello, Jo. You are prompt. That is good."

"Hello, Uncle Henry," Jo replied while leaning in and kissing her uncle's smooth, clean-shaven cheek. Uncle Henry was above average height, trim of build with a full head of gray hair. He worked as a clothier and his dress was impeccable. His manner was proper but his eyes reflected a kindness that often contradicted his careful cadence of speech. "Come in young lady. Do come in."

"How are you Uncle Henry?"

"Fine. Fine. The old bones are holding up quite well."

"Where is Aunt Bessie? Is she home yet?"

"Yes. Bessie just arrived home a few minutes ago. She is getting some tea ready and will be out promptly."

Uncle Henry led Jo to the formal living room. Everything was just as Jo remembered it. The same deep mahogany framed sofa with cream and brown nub textured silk faced two matching barrel chairs which made up the conversation area, and it was there that Jo and Henry made their way. Jo had visited often throughout the years and she always found it remarkable that life on Edge Road seemed to change not an iota from year to year. The end tables were clutter free as always although she saw a classic novel on the end table to the right of the sofa and a Life magazine sporting the top of the end table to the left of the sofa. Jo smiled as she took note that Uncle Henry was reading Ivanhoe again, and Aunt Bessie was up to date with the goings on in Life.

Before Jo had time to take a seat, Aunt Bessie walked into the room with a warm smile on her delicately proportioned face. She carried a doily laced tray with three cups and a small tea kettle. "Hello, my dear Jo. How are you?" She carefully lowered the tray to the oval table that fronted the sofa, and then she opened her arms for Jo who moved in for a big hug and kiss. Aunt Bessie, petite and unreserved in her displays of affection was a true complement to her husband who was tall though lean and profoundly reserved in speech and affection. Bessie was dressed in a tasteful floral print dress of yellows and greens. Bessie's entrance brightened the room and Jo's mood.

Bessie stepped back a pace and looked Jo up and down. "It is so wonderful to see you Jo. We are delighted you have come to visit. Look Henry – look at our lovely girl."

"Yes. She certainly is a beauty. I agree," smiled Henry.

Even though her aunt and uncle were very kind and Jo enjoyed their company, her rapidly pumping heart signaled the need to get right to the point of her visit. Trying to hide her unease, she smoothed her skirt and sat on the edge of the sofa. Folding her hands tightly in her lap, she took a deep breath and then blurted out the reason for the visit. "I find myself in a situation, and I have come to ask for your help."

"Go on dear," prodded Aunt Bessie slowly taking a seat in the chair opposite Jo as Uncle Henry looked on.

"I am rather embarrassed. I must start back a bit. I met a man, and I felt that I was in love." Jo had practiced what she would say, but the words would barely come as she looked into the eyes of her aunt. She knew that her news would shock and appall them, but she plowed ahead as she felt she must. "I let things get a bit out of hand and I find myself...." she hesitated at a loss. "I find myself...in...." Unable to continue, Jo stared down at her wringing hands.

"Let me help you," Aunt Bessie said gently. "Jo, are you with child?"

"Yes. I...am," Jo found she could not look up at either of them as she answered. Shaking, she waited for their reaction.

After a long moment, Aunt Bessie rushed over to Jo and enveloped her tightly and securely in her arms. Jo clung to Bessie for a good long while as tears of relief washed over her. Bessie's eyes had filled as well.

Minutes passed as Aunt Bessie comforted Jo, brushing away her tears and smoothing her hair. Uncle Henry remained quiet as he watched them. He thought of his brother William, Jo's father, and the fact that he would be extremely disappointed by the turn of events. Saddened, Henry felt that his brother's untimely demise may have contributed to the recklessness of his young daughter who needed guidance and protection. The world was a difficult and often cruel place for single pregnant women and

Jo would be forced to withstand disapproval from all around her. Uncle Henry was not happy, he felt that Jo certainly knew better and should have been able to handle herself more prudently even at her young age. She never should have succumbed to the baser urges and allowed her suitors such liberties, and he was appalled that Jo had discredited herself so. Henry was not a mean-spirited person, but he believed in propriety. Of course, he and Bessie would help Jo.

Filled with disappointment he asked, "Jo, will the boy who did this to you marry you?"

"No….. He cannot marry me. I just recently found out that he is married already. He never told me, and I had no idea!"

"Oh how dreadful. Poor Jo," breathed Aunt Bessie.

Taking charge, Henry stated, "Of course, your Aunt Bessie and I will help you and we will make sure you are cared for until the birth. Is that what you wished to ask of us?"

"Yes. Uncle Henry. It is. I am so sorry to bring this to your door. I understand your position and I am truly sorry to come to you this way, but I thank you. My boss, Dr. Brian, has already fired me, and I cannot afford my rent without a job. I really am so sorry."

"I am not surprised to hear that you have been fired. Pregnant unwed women are not very welcome in the workplace," Bessie paused. Slowly she asked, "Have you thought about adoption?"

"Yes….a bit. I have the number for the Jewish Adoption Center from the doctor who confirmed the pregnancy. I could call this week and make an appointment to discuss the possibility," she said hesitantly feeling that her aunt and uncle needed some proactive action from her in order to agree to house her.

"Good. That is a fine idea," said Henry. "When would you like to move in?"

"Would next week be okay?" Jo asked.

"Next week it is. We will ready a room for you. I will help you move your things," Henry offered.

"And I will be glad to accompany you to the Jewish Adoption Center for your meeting once you arrange it. All will be well Jo. We will help you get through this difficult and trying time," Bessie soothed.

"Thank you both. Your support means so much to me. I love you both."

Jo was relieved that the difficult discussion was done and beyond thankful for her generous aunt and uncle. She hugged and kissed both of them enthusiastically, and Aunt Bessie smiled as her proper husband squirmed.

The following week, Jo boxed up the contents of her room, bid goodbye to Mrs. Levinter and moved to 214 Edge Road. With a resounding bang, Jo physically and figuratively shut the door on her life of independence.

Chapter Eight

Mid July

A smile lighting her face, Sandra watched from the backdoor as Michael ran through the backyard on the way to his friend Bobbie's to play.

"Call me when you get to Bobbie's house," Sandra called before he reached the alley. As she turned away from the door, the telephone rang. She walked the few steps to the end of the tiny galley kitchen and picked it up. Her friend Barbara had news for her.

"I was thinking of you today and wanted to share something with you. I hope you will not find me at all presumptuous," began Barbara.

"That could never happen, Barbara. What is it? You have me curious."

"Well...I was in a meeting first thing this morning." Barbara worked for the Jewish agency in town as a well-respected social worker. Sandra had always been very proud of her friend, and she often wished that she had chosen sociology over English in her days at college.

"And," Sandra prompted.

"Today Jean gave a report on adoptions. She mentioned that this is the first time that we have a surplus of children waiting to be adopted. That has never been the case before."

"That is interesting."

"Yes. I thought so too. Please take this for how it is intended, I know that we don't speak about the difficulties you had after Michael was born, but just in case you and Jay have ever or would ever consider adoption this would be the perfect time to try. I know that you have wanted another child – you have shared that with me – this could be a great opportunity."

"I see," Sandra said. "How intriguing. I don't know...," she trailed off.

"Sandra, of course I am just suggesting."

"Barbara, no, no you misunderstand. I am very interested. Thank you so much for bringing it to my attention. What would we need to do if we were to proceed?"

"I will give you Jean's number. You can make an appointment to meet with her, and she will guide you through."

"Okay. Wait just a minute while I grab something to write on." Sandra ran around the kitchen looking for paper. She found a paper bag and thankfully a pen near the phone. For once, she thought. "Hello. I have paper. What are Jean's last name and her number, Barbara?"

"Jean Berman. Her number is Rogers 4 – 9999."

"Great. I have it. Thanks Barbara. You are a dear for thinking of us."

"Please let me know if you need any help. I better get back to work. I'll speak to you later."

The phone rang again as Sandra hung up with Barbara.

"Mom, have you been on the phone? I've been calling you to tell you I'm at Bobbie's just like you told me to."

"Oh, Michael! Good boy. Yes. I had a call. I am glad you are there. Have fun. Come home by 5:30 for dinner. Bobbie's mother will help you tell the time."

After Sandra hung up with Michael she plopped down in the chair by the phone and pondered Barbara's wonderful news. She decided to wait for Jay to come home from work rather than bothering him during his busy day to discuss the amazing development. A new baby, she thought. After all this time – could it truly be possible? She and Jay had wanted a large family, one bigger than each of them had had growing up, but Michael's birth had been complicated and Sandra's tubes had become blocked. Even after the failed, painful attempt to blow her tubes open, they had continued to hope and pray for a miracle. Eventually they had resigned themselves and had given up. Sandra felt that a closed door had suddenly swung open.

Jarred from her musings, Sandra jumped up and bumped her head on the phone cradle when her mother called from her bedroom next to the kitchen, "Sandra, when are we going to the store?"

"About ten minutes. I need to change first," Sandra replied rubbing her head.

It had been a very busy afternoon and Sandra had been glad to be busy, it had made the time until Jay came home much quicker. Jay usually did not make it home for dinner with the family, and this night was no exception. He did make it just in time to say goodnight to Michael.

Sandra reheated the chicken and rice the family had eaten a few hours previously and then she prepared a small salad for Jay's dinner while Jay read the newspaper. Sandra sat at their Arts and Crafts knockoff dining room table with Jay while he ate his meal. Throughout the day, Sandra had thought about the adoption possibility and she had grown very enthusiastic about it. She was confident that Jay would be interested as well, so she was surprised to find that she was nervous as she brought up the topic.

"Jay," she began carefully, "I had a very interesting call from Barbara today."

"How is Barbara?"

"She's fine."

"What was on her mind today?"

"She said that she had attended a meeting in the morning and found out that for the first time the Jewish Adoption Center has more children to be adopted than they have parents to adopt."

"Why is that?"

"I didn't think to ask and she didn't mention it," Sandra wondered if she should have asked. "Barbara wanted to let us know that this would be a good time to try to adopt a baby if that is something we were interested in doing."

"Hmmmm. We have not really talked about adopting except that one time."

"Yes. I remember. I think we thought it would be very difficult to do and too costly if we needed to go out of town. But when I got off the phone with Barbara I gave it a lot of thought. This is right in town. I think it's a great idea," she put forth. "What do you think?"

Jay absently rubbed his chin which was already stubbly even though he had shaved just that morning. Sandra held her breath. "You know what? I agree. You know how much I want another child. I think it's a remarkable idea," he said quickly warming to the concept. "Do you have the name of someone to meet with and get more specifics?"

"Yes, I do. Barbara gave me the name and number for the woman to contact. Should I call her tomorrow?" Sandra asked with growing excitement.

"Yes, call tomorrow. Make an appointment for first thing in the morning if you can – any morning next week would be fine," Jay said as he reached for Sandra's hand. Smoothly, he pulled her to her feet and twirled her around. He sang to her, his deep baritone off-key rendition of the Mills Brother's "Daddy's Little Girl" made her laugh out loud. He held her close as he sang, and they laughed and danced around the small dining room. "A new baby! What a great idea!" Jay exclaimed giving Sandra a big kiss filled with promise.

Sandra did call the Jewish Adoption Center the very next day, and she was able to get the first appointment for Tuesday morning.

***

Relieved that nausea has been replaced with extra energy and well-being, Jo faced new challenges as she neared the end of the first trimester of her pregnancy. She visited with Carol and Mrs. Rosen often and they continued to be a great source of encouragement and support. Mrs. Rosen explained that she would start to show significantly within a few weeks. At that point, things would get a great deal tougher, because people tended to be especially judgmental and outwardly disapproving of unwed pregnant young women. Carol and Mrs. Rosen worried for their friend. They were very pleased that Jo was safely

51

ensconced at her aunt and uncle's home for the duration of the pregnancy and delivery, or so they thought.

It is time, thought Jo. With the baby growing and the days and weeks moving forward, Jo knew that she needed to take the first step in the adoption process. It was a tremendous effort for her, because she already loved her baby. She had much time on her hands to reflect and envision the life within her, and she was constantly amazed at how close she felt and how often she spent thinking about her own mother and imagining what she would say. She wondered if things would have been different had her mother been there to help her through this episode of her life. Aunt Bessie and Uncle Henry regaled her with tales of her parents that she couldn't possibly know or remember, and she found the tales tremendously comforting.

With resolve and amazing fortitude, she retrieved the phone number from Dr. Goodman that was wedged deep inside the front pocket of her favorite pocketbook. With trembling hands and a splintering heart, she placed the call to the Jewish Adoption Center that she had been putting off and made an appointment for the following Tuesday to meet with a caseworker, Mrs. Berman. She checked with Aunt Bessie and fortuitously she was available to attend the appointment as well.

Chapter Nine

Tuesday arrived. Excitement filled the air as Sandra and Jay dressed for the important meeting. Jay chose to wear his charcoal work suit, although he opted to leave the shirt collar open and forego the tie, and Sandra dressed in a light cotton lime green dress with white heels and a small pillbox white hat.

"You look very nice, Sandra," he said as they walked to their car.

"Thank you, Jay. I want to make a good impression."

"I am sure you will, sweetheart," he said as he opened the passenger door of their blue Buick LeSabre for Sandra.

They drove the short ten-minute drive to the small brick building of the Jewish Adoption Center and entered the front door hand in hand. They were nervous and excited. Sandra had briefed Barbara about the meeting and she met them at the door with big hugs, then she led them to Mrs. Berman's office and made the introductions.

Sandra and Jay looked around the room and both smiled as they noticed the poster pictures of happy families. It seemed they had discussed adoption singularly for the past week. They were thrilled and excited about the prospect of expanding their family.

Mrs. Berman listened carefully and wrote detailed notes as Jay and Sandra Brenner openly answered questions about their child, Michael aged 6, their desire for more children but inability because of a medical condition, Jay's career as a manufacturing executive, Sandra's part–time teaching work, their home life with Sandra's blind mother, their large extended family, and even their synagogue affiliation. She found the couple mature and excellent prospective parents. They expressed enthusiasm but tempered it with understanding of the realities of bringing a non-biological child into their home. All in all, they were delightful.

Mrs. Berman retrieved a few papers from her desk. She slid one page across the table to Jay. "Here are the costs related to the adoption that you will incur if approved. I will step out a moment while you look them over."

Jay read over the itemized list. He smiled at Sandra and patted her hand to assure her that they would be able to handle it. Jay worked very hard for a large corporation but his salary was moderate, though respectable. The adoption costs had been a real worry for him over the past week. He had not shared this worry with Sandra. Jay nodded at Mrs. Berman as she reentered the room. They were moving forward.

"I think I have enough information for today. But, I need to make a home visit in the near future. I would like to meet Michael at that time, and then I will decide of your suitability as an adoptive family." As that statement sank in, Jay and Sandra both inadvertently straightened in their chairs.

"When would you like to come?" Sandra happily chimed as she checked the angle of her hat.

"Would next Monday work for you?"

"Do you need me home as well?" Jay asked.

"Yes. That is required."

"Could we make it first thing in the morning again?" he requested.

"Yes. That would work for me. How is 9:00am?"

Jay and Sandra nodded. "Yes that will be fine. We will have Michael ready to meet you," Sandra said.

"Very good then. We are set." After shaking Mrs. Berman's hand, Jay took Sandra's arm and led her from the room.

As they excitedly left the building, Sandra noticed a pretty young girl in a navy dress and low-heeled shoes accompanied by an older finely dressed woman in a stunning cream tailored suit, possibly her mother, pass them on the path. What a pretty young woman. She looks so sad, thought Sandra fleetingly.

***

Tuesday had arrived much too quickly for Jo. Nodding politely to the handsome couple she and Jo passed, Aunt Bessie reached for Jo's hand. Together they continued walking slowly up the path to the small two story nondescript brick building with only a small name plate by the front door identifying it as the Jewish Adoption Center.

"All will be fine, Jo," Aunt Bessie said softly, "you are doing the right thing."

Jo briefly looked over at her aunt and forced a small smile.

Mrs. Berman, the caseworker, introduced herself and Jo introduced Aunt Bessie as Mrs. Bessie Engle to Mrs. Berman. Once the introductions were concluded Mrs. Berman led them from the waiting area and down a long hallway. Her door was the last one on the right side. As they settled into the two seats across from Mrs. Berman who moved toward her seat behind her desk, Jo noticed the room was decorated with many poster pictures of happy families with babies in their arms. Her stomach tightened and tears welled as she noticed one particular mother who looked a bit like herself holding a beautiful baby girl in a tiny pink outfit. She clasped her hands together in her lap and willed herself not to let the tears fall as her eyes remained fixed on the picture.

Having noticed Jo's behavior, Mrs. Berman cleared her throat and then began the questioning.

"Miss Engle, Mrs. Engle, Are you here today to discuss adoption?"

Jo tore her eyes away from the upsetting picture, straightened in her chair and answered, "I'm not sure."

"I believe we are." Aunt Bessie stated. "We love you very much Jo, but you alone will have a home with us after the baby is born. Not the baby."

Stunned, Jo looked quickly at her aunt and then down to her tightly clasped hands in her lap. She remained silent.

Recognizing the tension, Mrs. Berman lowered her eyes to Jo's stomach and noticed the slight bulge.

"When is your baby due, Miss Engle?"

"In January."

"Have you confirmed this with a doctor?"

"Yes. Dr. Goodman."

"Is the father of the baby involved at all in this decision?"

"No. Is that a problem?"

"No. Unfortunately it's a common happenstance."

It saddened Jo to think about the many others before her who had to handle this without the father of their children. As her thoughts started to wander in that direction, she pulled herself back to the discussion at hand. With trembling voice, she inquired, "How would the adoption be handled?"

Mrs. Berman took a breath and then began what must have been a speech that she had made too many times before. "I will be the caseworker for you and your baby and today if you decide to proceed, I'll ask you some necessary questions about yourself, your background, and your family the answers of which I'll record in your file. I will review the applications of possible adoptive parents. I personally interview and perform home visits to prospective parents to determine that the living conditions are acceptable. I'll match your baby once it's born with suitable adoptive parents. At the time the baby is born, I will add the baby's information to the file. The baby will be taken from the hospital and put into a foster home for three months. In that time, he or she will be monitored and I'll follow the baby's progress. When the baby has reached certain milestones in eating and sleeping and the waiting time period has expired, he or she will be officially adopted and the adoptive parents that were chosen will take the baby home."

"Will I be told the names of the adoptive parents?" Jo stammered overwhelmed by all the information.

"No. And they will not be told yours. The adoption will be closed which means that information will not be shared among the parties. In addition, once the adoption is finalized, the baby's birth certificate will be sealed and only the adoption information will be available."

"So, I won't know anything about the baby?" Jo asked while holding her breath. The stark realization that she was mentally and emotionally ill-prepared slammed into her with sudden impact.

"No. The information of each side is kept private. That is for the safety of all concerned. You will be free to move on with your life."

"But what if I want to find the baby one day or the baby wants to find me?"

"Miss Engle," Mrs. Berman stated with emphasis, "Why are you here thinking about putting your baby up for adoption?"

"I want the baby to be raised by two parents with lots of love. That is my wish," she responded with a quiver.

"Good. And... You have no husband and you cannot adequately provide for the baby. Is that correct?"

"Yes that's true," she whispered glancing at her aunt whose gaze remained fixed on Mrs. Berman.

"We can help you to make sure your baby is provided for. That's what we do here. I'll make sure that your baby has those things for the sake of you and for your baby, but in order to do that you must give up the right to your baby. You must allow him or her to be secure in their new home and you must go on with your life."

"I understand," Jo responded miserably as she felt her options dwindling.

Let's proceed then. Please answer all my questions as thoroughly as you can. Full name?"

"Jo Engle."

"Miss Engle, are you Jewish?"

"Yes."

"Your mother was Jewish as well?"

"Yes."

"Did you receive any Jewish education?"

"Yes. I went to Hebrew School and I was Bas Mitzvahed. I was raised in a traditional home and attended an Orthodox synagogue."

"Your age and birthdate?"

"20, July 14, 1942. My birthday was three days ago."

"Happy Birthday," intoned Mrs. Berman.

"Thank you."

"Marital Status?"

"Single."

"Education?"

"I graduated from high school and have taken some college classes. I'm on leave from college now."

The questions continued and Jo shared her parents' names, their birth dates, dates of death, causes of death, and the fact that she was an only child.

"Anything you would like to share about the father of the baby?"

"No, nothing at all," Jo replied firmly.

Carefully making a notation about Jo's resolute decision concerning the father, Mrs. Berman redirected the conversation. "Very well. Let's discuss the months of pregnancy. We highly recommend you stay at Kritt Place, a home for unwed mothers located nearby. We can work on getting you in as early as next month."

"I don't want to go there!" Jo said emphatically shaking her head for emphasis. "I heard that if you go there, you're forced to give your baby up for adoption."

"Who told you that?"

"Friends."

"That's not the truth. The facility is highly recommended because young girls in your situation should be around other young girls. The staff is properly trained for your special circumstances."

Jo turned to Aunt Bessie and pleaded, "Please don't make me go there!"

Aunt Bessie and Mrs. Berman shared a meaningful look. They had discussed the need for Jo to be in such an environment and they were in accord on the issue.

"I will take you there to look it over and then we will decide," Aunt Bessie stated.

"I see," Jo replied helplessly.

"It will be for the best. You'll see," said Mrs. Berman.

"Do I have to sign anything for adoption now?" Jo asked resignation evident in her slumped posture and defeated tone.

"No. That will be done after the baby is born."

"Will I be able to see the baby in the hospital if I decide to put him or her up for adoption?"

"Yes, if you wish you'll be able to see and care for the baby after the birth while in the hospital."

"That's good," Jo responded with a glimmer of relief at the thought of at least seeing the baby and spending some time with him or her in the hospital. Possibly she still had time to make the final decision, although she recognized that everyone around her had already decided.

***

The following week, the home visit went very well for the Brenner family. Mrs. Berman noted that Michael was a well-adjusted though highly energetic boy, the home was large and casually furnished, the grandmother enthusiastic about the possibility of a new addition to the family, and the Brenner family quite suitable.

"What is the next step?" Jay inquired of Mrs. Berman.

"Once officially approved we will wait for the baby to be born, and then I will match you up. At your request, we will try to match you with a baby girl. We have a number of babies due in the short term."

"Will we be able to take the baby home right from the hospital?" Sandra asked hopefully.

"No. You will not see the baby in the hospital. There is a waiting period in which the baby will be put in a foster home. Once the baby is three months old and has reached certain milestones in sleeping and eating, I will contact you and we will arrange for you to pick her up at my office."

Concerned, Jay inquired, "Will we be told when the baby is born and her progress?"

"Yes. I will notify you of the birth and you may call to find out the baby's progress. I will keep you apprised. Speak to you soon. Good bye for now."

Chapter Ten

Fall 1962

Waiting for the birth was excruciating for Jo. She missed her college life and friends and she felt completely dependent as she hunkered down and watched life go by from her rightmost bedroom window, reminiscent of days long before when mourning as a young child for her mother. The trees turned reds and oranges and golden yellows and then finally brown, which filled her with much sadness, as she witnessed the bleak landscape transition toward winter. It brought home the bleakness of her life and the fact that as she got closer to seeing the beautiful life within her, she also faced the probability that she would need to give her child to others and move on with her own life. She may have been very young in years, but Jo had seen much and she bore the marks of all the misfortune that she had weathered. Her outward sweetness masked the scars of all her losses and her situation was creating a new, raw wound that she was certain would never completely heal.

She was still welcome at Carol's house and Jo was grateful that her friend had not ostracized her unlike many others. One particularly dismal afternoon, she went for a visit. Mrs. Rosen's favorite Aunt Sarah was visiting as well. Jo had met Aunt Sarah on several past occasions, at family functions formal as well as informal, and she liked the outgoing, jovial woman with the outrageous bold attire. Aunt Sarah was big in all ways, personality, stature and certainly her dress. She often sported the boldest prints one could imagine and the wildest accessories accumulated from her travels throughout the world. Won over by all with her zest for life and fascinating stories of distant lands and cultures, she was just the person to brighten Jo's day.

Aunt Sarah greeted Jo with a big hug and kiss. Noticing Jo's pregnant belly, she quirked a brow in question. "Well hello Jo, I see we have much to catch up on," she said with a warm smile as she arranged herself on the sofa.

"Hello Aunt Sarah, yes I guess so."

"Sit right down next to me, and let's chat. I want to hear all," Aunt Sarah said motioning Jo to the seat next to her on the couch.

Jo was comfortable with Aunt Sarah and it felt good to share her story with someone non-judgmental. "My story is simple and sad, Aunt Sarah. I wish it was different. I met a man while at college, and I truly thought we were in love even though we had been dating a short time. He made me feel special and loved, but he was not truthful, and I was completely wrong about him. Once he figured out I was pregnant, before I even knew myself, he was gone!" she said quickly.

"Oh my my, that is just terrible," Aunt Sarah said as she put her arm around the young, vulnerable girl. "When is the baby due?"

"In January."

"You still have some time then. What are you planning to do about the baby?"

"My Aunt Bessie and Uncle Henry have made it clear that I can live with them after the baby is born only if I give up the baby for adoption. I don't really seem to have a choice, because I can't afford to care for the baby on my own. But I already love my baby, and I'm miserable with this decision," she explained as her eyes became glassy with tears.

"I'm sure you are," Aunt Sarah said clasping Jo's hand in her two hands.

"More than anything I want this child to have two parents who love him or her. As you know, I grew up without my mother, and it was so hard for me. I needed her so much. My father was a good man, but I needed both of them. I sincerely want my baby to have two parents. I'm heartbroken that I can't provide that."

"What a big decision for such a young girl," Aunt Sarah said, hugging Jo tightly to her ample chest. "It sounds to me like you have started to make your decision."

"I don't want to."

"Yes. But you will. How are you holding up physically?"

"I'm feeling good, but the waiting is so hard. How am I going to survive this?"

"You will. I know you will. I know a bit about that myself."

"Really?"

Aunt Sarah paused and considered, "I have a story to tell you, Jo. I think my story may help you. The moral of my story is that you will go on and you will live your life, because you must."

"What story? I'm intrigued."

"Jo" began Aunt Sarah, "the story I'm about to impart is difficult for me to share, but I do so because I believe it will help you to see that you can and must overcome this adversity. There are people we encounter whose actions truly alter the course of our lives causing us great difficulty but also forcing us to find ways to accommodate the changes and persevere.

Apprehensively but also immensely curious Jo waited for Aunt Sarah to go on.

"I was eighteen during the Great War, which was later known as World War I. One Saturday night, I went to a dance at the school near our home. Many of the boys were on leave from the navy and I met one such man, a handsome sailor named Willy. He said that I took his breath away when he saw me standing in my best dress which was a calf-length, rose-colored dress with white overlay that I had sewn myself."

"Ahh..," she sighed as she remembered, and Jo smiled as she watched the happy transformation on Aunt Sarah's face as she relived the fond memories.

"Back to my story... Willy sauntered over and my heart literally stopped. He had on his uniform and looked so dapper. We danced more dances together that night than was appropriate, and I felt wonderful. He acted quite the gentleman and at the end of the evening asked if he could escort me home. I was thrilled, and so we slowly walked the short distance to my home."

"That sounds very romantic, Aunt Sarah," Jo said as she took a bite of a cracker she found on the table.

"Yes. I had never felt so admired. It was a heady feeling! To add to that, the very next day, Willy appeared at my door with a bouquet of flowers. My mother was remarkably surprised when she opened the door and found such a handsome man bringing her daughter flowers. He asked if I was free for a walk, and I gladly changed into a walking outfit and joined him for a good long walk. My mother and sister decided to chaperone, and they walked a distance behind. It was all so exciting! Each day that week, Willy came to my house and brought a present. He stayed for meals with us and before I knew it, I had fallen in love. He only had two more weeks of leave, and then he was returning to Europe. A whirlwind romance, my mother kept saying."

"The beginning of the second week of our courtship, Willy asked my father for my hand in marriage. Of course, everyone was shocked by the suddenness, but stranger things have happened during wartime. My father gave his blessing and I gave my consent, and then the whole house was in an uproar as we prepared for a wedding in just six short days. I was deliriously happy! Willy and I spent every moment together except for those spent on wedding preparations. Being one of the youngest siblings came in handy, because my married sisters and their spouses jumped in and helped as much as they could. My mother and sisters were unstoppable."

"It sounds like a fairy tale!" Jo exclaimed. "What an amazing story!"

"It was the most wonderful time of my life!" continued Aunt Sarah. "The wedding was held on our back lawn that Sunday, and it was truly magical. It was a gorgeous June day with not a cloud in the sky, my mother's wedding dress had been altered just so and it fit me to perfection, the food was delicious and plentiful and the most important thing was that my handsome Willy stood up with me in formal attire including a top hat. He looked smashing. We made a remarkable looking couple. It was truly the happiest day of my life!"

"To give us newlyweds some privacy, my parents and sister spent the first week of our married life at my sister Hannah's house. We played house and had so much fun. Of course, we spent every moment together. But all too soon the week and leave were over, and Willy's ship sailed from the harbor. My mother stood with me as I waved and waved goodbye to my new husband, my love. I wrote letter after letter filled with sweet words and scented with perfume sending all my love across the ocean. Knowing it would take quite some time, I waited for his letters to arrive but none ever did."

"The war ended in November, and I was thrilled knowing that soon he would come home to me. But the days turned into weeks, and I watched the other soldiers and navy men return home. I would try to be happy for their wives and girlfriends, but I was heartsick. The weeks turned into months. I sent letter after letter to the navy office inquiring if he was injured or worse dead, but the letters returned in the negative. Willy had been discharged unscathed. The months turned into a year, and now incredibly it has been over 45 years since I have seen or heard from my husband William."

Hugging Aunt Sarah, tears streamed down Jo's face. She had no words for such a heartbreaking story. Could this really be Aunt Sarah's life? She was truly an amazing person with a constant smile and kind words, someone who was always optimistic and encouraging.

"Aunt Sarah, I'm so very sorry. I never knew!"

"Well dear, I don't tell my sad story often. I am quite embarrassed by the fact that I was duped by a handsome, honey-tongued man such as him."

"How could you have known?"

"I don't know, Jo. Through the years, I have thought over every word we shared, and I just don't know. He worked on my innocence, and I have paid the price. I never re-married and I never had children."

"It's so tragic."

"I shared this story not to sadden you Jo, but instead to give you strength to do what you must with the adoption and then move on. If I was able to muster through, I know you will as well."

"Thank you so much for sharing it with me, Aunt Sarah. I do understand."

***

For Sandra, time was also dragging. Jay had his work to keep him busy and although Sandra had Michael, her mother, and the house to fill her time, she found she was immensely anxious. She was nervous about the caseworker visits and if their family would be found suitable. She was worried about Michael's behavior and how he would behave with the new baby. Seven years age difference was significant, and she was concerned about the challenges they would face with two such disparately aged children. Lastly and overwhelmingly, she wondered how she would feel about this child, would she be able to love her unconditionally as her own. This was not a given and it became a daily concern. She didn't dare mention this last worry to anyone, including Barbara, because she believed they would think her horrible. Over the months of waiting, it became her secret and greatest fear.

Barbara had been Sandra's rock through the whole process and even though things had gone smoothly each step of the way, there was Barbara with encouraging words and great advice.

"Barbara, we just got the news! The caseworker has officially approved us," Sandra fairly sang into the phone. It was late November and Sandra was bursting. She had called Jay, but his secretary said he was out, and she would have him return the call on his return. Sandra just had to tell someone immediately.

"That's wonderful! I'm so happy for you and Jay!" Barbara exclaimed. "What else did she say?"

"They have a few babies with due dates in January. If all goes well...." Sandra trailed off.

"Oh how exciting. This is great news. How did Jay react?"

"Well, I feel guilty, because I called his office but he was out. I couldn't wait, so I called you. You're the first to know! Please don't tell anyone just yet."

"I'm honored. Of course, I'll keep your confidence. This is so exciting! Have you been thinking of names?"

"Not yet. Nothing was for certain until now. Oh Barbara, the waiting has been difficult so far, however will we make it another four or more months."

"You will. I'll help you. Mazal Tov, Sandra."

"Thank you for everything, Barbara. I have to go. Michael should be coming home soon."

Jay and Sandra excitedly shared the news with many of their close friends and all the extended family. Expectation, excitement, yet anxiety ruled the day as they waited for the baby's birth.

Chapter Eleven

Jo attended counseling sessions with Mrs. Berman throughout the summer and early fall. Their discussions focused primarily on Jo's ability to handle her current situation and plans for her future. Aunt Bessie and Uncle Henry were very kind and affectionate, but their son and daughter, Mitchell and Agnes, were irate that Jo was staying with them. Even though married and no longer living in the home with Bessie and Henry, the children berated their parents continually for harboring Jo and her indecency. Pained, Jo had often overheard their hateful rants.

Jo sincerely wanted to move back in with her step-mother, Anna, but Anna's mother was ill and needed all the attention that Anna could muster. In addition, Anna's mother was not overly fond of Jo for reasons unbeknownst to Jo. With that door closed, Mrs. Berman finally convinced Jo to move to Kritt Place for her final months of pregnancy. It was the usual protocol for young unwed pregnant women handled by the Jewish Adoption Center, and Mrs. Berman was very pleased that Jo had finally been brought to heel. She was additionally happy that Jo wanted to help pay for her stay there demonstrating some real sense of responsibility and accountability. The agency would pay the balance.

On October 1, Jo was scheduled to move to Kritt Place. Jo awoke from a restless sleep, groggy and sober with puffy eyes and mottled skin. She had cried herself to sleep once again. Desperately wanting to put off the inevitable, she checked over the few belongings that she would take with her.

She dressed slowly, exhaustion evident in every movement. Aunt Bessie entered the room after a gentle knock that went unanswered, and found Jo sitting on the edge of the bed staring into space. "We should leave shortly, dear. The administrator said she would meet us at the front entrance at 9:00."

"I'm ready," Jo responded as she slowly rose. Her words in no way meshed with the terrified expression on her mottled but lovely face.

"Have you eaten any breakfast?" Aunt Bessie asked quietly as she noticed the physical effects of Jo's distress displayed all over her features. They must keep to the plan, Aunt Bessie thought.

"No. I'm not at all hungry," Jo replied shaking her head.

"Well. You need to eat and the baby needs to eat as well. What about a piece of toast and some tea?"

"Ok. I guess I should."

After obediently eating the small breakfast, the two made their way the short driving distance to Kritt Place. Jo sat stoically in the car throughout the ride staring straight ahead, body rigid, tears threatening. She desperately wanted to manage for the sake of her kind aunt and uncle, because she fully understood that they needed her to make this move. Their children, Agnes and Mitchell, continued in their daily phone calls and frequent visits to voice intense disapproval of Jo's presence in their parents' home and lives, and it created extreme discord in the family. "She's like poison to this family flaunting her pregnancy and showing no embarrassment!" Agnes had screamed at her parents just the day before knowing full well that Jo was within hearing distance. Hurt beyond words, Jo suffered. She loved her aunt and uncle and felt safe with them, but the cousins made the situation untenable. She needed to be gone. Head bowed, she reached for her aunt's hand as they headed into the home for unwed pregnant girls.

Mrs. Grant, the woman in charge of the facility met them at the door with a cheerful smile. "Mrs. Engle, Miss Engle, since we completed most of the paperwork when you visited back in July, we can finish the rest later. Let's make our way to Jo's room. I think you will find it most comfortable."

Kritt Place was a two story red brick building built around the turn of the century in the colonial style. At any given time, there may have been up to 30 residents living there "hiding" during their pregnancies while preserving the sensibilities of proper society. On the day Jo arrived, there were 27 and she made 28. Girls were sent to Kritt Place from all over the county, forced from their homes by "loving" family members who were inclined to protect their own names and reputations. One such girl, Beverly, was Jo's roommate, a pretty blond in her last month of pregnancy.

Upon reaching the room, they saw Beverly exiting as they approached. "Jo, this is Beverly West, your roommate," introduced Mrs. Grant.

"Hello Beverly. Nice to meet you," managed Jo with a small smile.

"Nice to meet you too. I'm off to do my chores. See you later," Beverly replied sweetly.

Jo moved her suitcase and toiletry bag to the unused side of the room. She looked around the functional space and began unpacking a few things as Aunt Bessie and Mrs. Grant made small talk. Jo didn't follow their conversation. She was lost in her own depressing thoughts. Before long, Aunt Bessie turned to leave. She hugged and kissed Jo, reminding her that she and Uncle Henry loved her very much and wanted the best for her. Jo returned the hug, hanging on for an extra bit.

"Take some time settling in and then in a half hour, come down to the communal area. I will look for you then and take you around to meet some of the girls. Lunch will follow," Mrs. Grant instructed. "I'll see you then."

"Okay. Thank you," Jo replied quietly.

"I'll show you out Mrs. Engle. Jo should do very well here," Jo heard Mrs. Grant say as the two made their way down the hallway. Exhausted from her ordeal, Jo slumped on her new bed.

Jo attempted to make her way at Kritt Place. She was her kind, gentle self but she could not rouse herself from her misery and sense of loneliness and abandonment. She tried to be friendly with Beverly but lapsed into tears at every effort. Mrs. Berman came to visit her and found her disconsolate. Within a week, Mrs. Grant was on the phone with Aunt Bessie.

"Jo does not appear to be settling in very well," Mrs. Grant began.

"Whatever is the problem?" Aunt Bessie questioned.

"She's extremely lonely. I've tried to get some of the other girls to befriend her, but she is not able to make the effort. Mrs. Berman agrees that she is not adjusting properly. Possibly Jo should return to your home briefly and regroup and then we can see," Mrs. Grant suggested.

"Of course. That is how it should be. Should I come pick her up later today?"

"Yes. After lunch would be best. I'll notify Jo and have her packed and ready."

"Thank you, Mrs. Grant. I'm sorry Jo has been a bother."

"Not at all. She is just a very sad young lady. Please be in touch in a few weeks."

Jo was packed and happily waiting when Aunt Bessie came to take her home. She truly smiled for the first time all week as she gratefully thanked her Aunt Bessie.

During the following month, Aunt Bessie, Uncle Henry and Mrs. Berman nurtured Jo as they continued to discuss the need for her to be ensconced at Kritt Place. They delved deeply into her loneliness issue and promised to make themselves available more by phone and visits.

In November, Jo took up residence at Kritt Place once again. Mrs. Berman appealed to her step-mother Anna to make an effort to visit. Anna had previously maintained that she could not stand to see Jo in such a place, but with repeated appeals and for Jo's well-being, Anna acquiesced. Jo was delighted and Anna's visit was pivotal in her acceptance of her situation. This time, Jo thrived, made friends, and accepted her confinement.

Chapter Twelve

January 1963

The time had finally come. Jo woke early in the morning with energy and expectation. By mid-day, she began to feel strange sensations and by nightfall, she knew she was in labor. At her prenatal checkup the week before, the doctor at Forest Hospital had told her that the baby was coming soon. He had explained what she would feel and what she should do. As instructed, Jo packed a small hospital bag with essentials, called her Aunt Bessie and found Mrs. Grant in her office. Shortly after, she was transported to Forest Hospital.

As Aunt Bessie and Uncle Henry made their way to the hospital, Bessie nervously inquired, "All will be well, will it not?"

"Yes. Everything will be fine. Jo will manage very well. She is a strong girl," Henry said trying to convince himself as well as Bessie. Though Bessie and Henry had already been blessed with two beautiful grandchildren, they were very aware that even in 1963 a safe birth was not a given. Bessie and Henry tried not to dwell on the fact that Jo's mother, Bessie's sister, had suffered a difficult delivery with Jo. Although her poor health had certainly been a contributing factor, things could and did go seriously wrong during the birth process, and they were suitably nervous as they waited.

Meanwhile, Jo faired well; her labor progressed at a moderate rate with no complications and lasting just short of 17 hours. Her burden was reduced with the help of anesthesia and she succumbed to it readily. A baby girl, 6lbs. 2 oz. was delivered at 11:53 am. In the early afternoon, Jo woke feeling very rested and alert. Looking to her right, she noticed a nurse entering the room.

"Hello Miss Engle. I'm Nurse Stephens. Would you like me to bring your baby in? We were not sure if you wished to see her."

"Yes. Please, please. I do with all my heart."

"Very well, I'll be right back. She is quite hungry."

I have a daughter Jo realized and smiled. If anyone had been looking they would have seen her face light up with a huge smile that was quickly tamped down by the sad thoughts that followed.

"She's so beautiful," Jo whispered awestruck as the nurse handed her the baby. She pulled the baby close and gently kissed her tiny head.

"Yes, she is," replied the nurse. If you feel ready, you should feed her. She's hungry," Nurse Stephens said holding up the bottle she had brought for emphasis.

"Oh. Would you show me how? I've never fed a baby before."

"Of course. Cradle the baby in your right arm with her head like so," Nurse Stephens instructed as she lifted the baby and adjusted her on Jo's right side. "Hold the bottle gently at an angle."

With ease, Jo did as she was told and the baby sucked happily. As Jo fed the baby she murmured close by her ear, "My little girl, my little girl, I'll love you forever." She closed her eyes tightly and willed herself to hold back the flood of tears that threatened to start and never stop. Jo focused on the truth. This was her little girl and she would love her forever no matter what she was forced to do. While the little baby drank, her mother drank as well. She drank in and memorized every detail of her tiny face impressing it on her memory for all the days and years to follow.

Anna, Jo's stepmother made a visit to the hospital. "I think she resembles Louisa," she told Jo. "I don't know if you are aware that I met your mother once shortly after she and William were married. This little girl," she said indicating the baby in Jo's arms "has her delicate features."

Shortly after, Carol and Mrs. Rosen arrived bringing a small teddy bear for the baby and a bigger one for her mother. "This must be so hard for you, Jo," Carol said hugging Jo then handing her the bears. "I don't know how you'll be able to give her up!"

"Babies are a great deal of work ladies," Mrs. Rosen reminded them sparing a stern look for Carol, "and very expensive. Women without husbands have an especially hard time my dears."

The next day, Uncle Henry and Aunt Bessie brought candy for Jo. "Have you called Mrs. Berman to tell her that you have decided on the adoption?" Aunt Bessie asked.

"Not yet," Jo replied sadly as she tightened her grip on the baby cradled in her arms. "I know it's what must be done," she said slowly as she looked at Aunt Bessie for confirmation. "I know that I have no choice." Her uncle and aunt nodded in recognition that her words were true but remained silent. As they gazed down into the dark eyes of the beautiful baby girl, they were deeply saddened. Their little great-niece must be raised by another family.

Jo continued to bond with the baby throughout the next few days in the hospital. Each day was bittersweet with its wonderment but with the knowledge that the end of their time together was fast approaching. Succumbing to the familial pressure and realizing that she truly could not care for the baby properly, Jo informed Mrs. Berman of her decision to put the baby up for adoption during the caseworker's visit in the hospital. Crying herself to sleep each night, Jo wished with all her heart that things were different. If only she was married with a good man by her side, she would never choose to give up her baby.

Near the end of the week, Nurse Stephens handed Jo a birth certificate form to fill in.

Remembering the meeting when Mrs. Berman had explained that the adoptive parents would choose the baby's name and all official records would use the name they chose, Jo reached for the form with unsteady fingers, "I didn't think I would be allowed to name my baby," she said.

"It is hospital procedure," the nurse replied smiling. "Go ahead."

Grasping the opportunity, Jo decided that she did indeed want to name her baby. Absently rubbing her chin, Jo mulled over her name choices. She took the matter very seriously. Naming a baby is significant, she thought. In the Jewish religion she remembered from her studies, God is believed to help the parents choose the name of the child, and the child is believed to manifest some traits from his or her name. Although the name she picked would likely be changed and never known to the baby, she proceeded to make her choice. With shaking hands and tears streaming once again down her face, she filled in the baby's name as Louisa Engle in loving memory of her mother. Harkening to the words of her step-mother, she hoped the baby would be like her mother in actions as well as appearance.

***

Mrs. Berman called Sandra from her office subsequent to her visit with Jo. "Mrs. Brenner, I have good news. We have matched you with a beautiful baby girl born three days ago."

"Oh my. What marvelous news! How big is she? Is she healthy?"

"She's perfect. 6lbs 2oz and very pretty with dark hair and eyes."

"That's wonderful! When can we see her?"

"I'm afraid you have a bit of a wait. As we discussed, there's a three month waiting period. The birth mother has given her verbal consent and she's scheduled to come to my office early next week, after her release from the hospital, to sign the voluntary foster home agreement forms. I'll call you again when the baby is settled in the foster home."

"Do you have a foster home picked out?"

"Yes. The family is very special and they have handled many of our children. She will be well-cared for."

After thanking Mrs. Berman, Sandra immediately called Jay at the office with the amazing news. Delighted, he decided to shorten his work day and take Sandra out for dinner at their favorite Italian restaurant. With soft candlelight reflecting off their beaming faces, they immensely enjoyed the deliciously rich rigatoni and tortellini dishes cooked to perfection as they celebrated the baby's birth and health. With lifted wine glasses, they toasted a bright future. Animatedly, they considered different names. None seemed perfect, so the decision was put off for another day. More urgently, the final wait had begun. It was time to tell Michael.

Chapter Thirteen

February 1963

On Mill Street, family members including grandparents, great aunts and uncles, aunts and uncles and cousins as well as a few of Michael's friends came to celebrate Michael's seventh birthday. The compact living room and dining room areas filled in no time. Michael was positioned by the door. He was responsible for taking everyone's coat upstairs. The arrival of Grandma Rena and Grandpa Jules found Michael jumping into Grandpa's arms laughing. Grandpa Jules swung him around and gave him a big bear hug. Grandpa Jules stood 6'2" and resembled all the men of his family - big boned, strong, and physical although his ongoing fight with cancer consistently took a very real toll and it showed. Until recently he had sported a quarterback football player's physique. Currently, his slightly outdated gray suit did not fit as precisely as it once had. Winded, Jules put Michael down, but reached into his depths and found the energy to join Michael in the grandfather-grandson fake punching routine they shared reminiscent of Grandpa Jules days as a youth boxing in private clubs throughout Baltimore. Jules had been an excellent boxer who succeeded in keeping himself and his two brothers in pocket money with his winnings.

Grandma Rena, who was petite and proper in her navy suit and pillbox hat, put a stop to their shenanigans. "Enough boys," she remonstrated with a stern look that didn't quite reach the smile in her eyes, thereby contradicting her words. Leaving the happy pair, Grandma Rena made her way through the room. Jay smiled as his mother walked toward him.

"Mother, how are you?" asked Jay warmly as he looked up from the drink he was pouring and kissed her cheek.

"It is a good day today, Jay," Grandma Rena said, nodding toward Jules and referring to his health. "I am just fine, thank you. I just cannot believe our Michael is seven already. How the years have flown?"

"Yes they have Mother. Sandra and I were just saying the same thing earlier today."

"Where is Sandra?" Grandma Rena asked as she looked around the room.

"Just coming in from the kitchen," Jay responded glimpsing Sandra in the dining room with a plate of lox.

"I'll go see if I can help her," Grandma Rena said as she moved into the dining room area and met up with Sandra.

"Hello Mother Brenner. How are you?"

"Fine, just fine. And you?"

"I am well. How is Jules?"

"He is managing. That is the best I can say. I'm glad he was able to make it to the party today."

"We are all delighted, Michael especially. He treasures his time with his grandfather."

"I know. They are quite the pair. You have made a beautiful spread, Sandra," praised Grandma Rena as she motioned to the bagels, lox, tuna salad, deviled eggs, cheeses, and juices arranged on the table before them. "Do you need me to help with anything?"

"Thank you. No, I am just about done. I think almost everyone has arrived. We will probably start in just a few minutes."

"Wonderful. I'll go over and speak to your mother, Sandra. She is looking well."

"Yes, she is. Thank you."

Rena greeted Grandma Lil with a kiss.

Michael quit his command post at the door once his friends Bobby, Johnny and Larry appeared. They each grabbed a plate of food from the table and then ran up the stairs headed to Michael's room.

Sandra called up to Michael. "Take your cousin Abby with you, Michael!"

Michael grumbled a bit to his friends, but he obediently went back downstairs and grabbed five year old Abby by the hand. Up the stairs they went. Children's noise was heard upstairs as the kids played with Michael's toys, but Abby appeared back downstairs a short time later complaining that the boys had pulled her blond piggy tails. She contented herself playing dolls with her three year old little sister, Amy, as her mother Marge looked on.

The guests sang a loud and off-key rendition of "Happy Birthday", and Michael blew out his candles with great gusto. Everyone laughed as he almost blew the chocolate-frosted homemade cake over. Excited to open his presents, Michael steadily made his way through the crowd to get to the pile on the end table. Curiously, he caught a fragment of his uncle and father deep in conversation about a baby girl as he passed by.

"How is the baby doing?" asked Uncle Robert.

"She's eating and sleeping very well," Jay replied.

Michael moved past but wondered who had a baby. His youngest baby cousin was Craig, Uncle Robert's son. His uncle Danny and Aunt Faith also had one son. No one had a baby girl. He shrugged and then turned his attention to the presents, quickly forgetting the exchange.

As Michael prepared for bed later that night, he gazed across the room at all the neat presents he had received that day. The coolest by far was the red Schwinn sting-ray bike with the banana seat his parents had given him.

As Jay entered the room, Michael looked up with a huge smile.

"Thanks for the coolest bike ever, Dad," he gushed.

"You are welcome. Your mother and I both know how big you are getting and that a big boy really needs a way to get around."

"I can't wait 'til it gets warmer to go, go, go! Why did I have to be born in February? It's such a cold, yucky month."

"I know it's hard to wait, but not all winter days are too cold. On nicer days, you can go out and practice riding in the alley." Alleyways ran through the development where the Brenner family lived and a good long alley ran right behind their house. The front of the house was rarely used by the family, because a busy road ran on the front side of the house and the back had driving access by the alley. Kids throughout the neighborhood availed themselves of the easy access through the alleys that connected their houses to those of their buddies.

"You should be ready by spring to ride all the way to Bobby's house," Jay said as he motioned to Sandra who was leaning against the doorframe.

"Oh boy!" Michael yelled enthusiastically.

Sandra padded quietly into the room and sat on the edge of Michael's bed. Jay grabbed a desk chair and pulled it next to the bed. "Michael," Jay began, "we have something big to tell you."

Michael quieted down quickly because his Dad sounded so serious.

"You know that Mom and I love you very, very much?"

"Yeah," Michael answered making a goofy face at the mushy words.

"Well we have even more love to share and we know that you do too."

"What?"

"What I mean is... You are going to be a big brother soon. You are going to have a baby sister."

"A baby sister?" Michael questioned. He was more than a bit confused as he looked at his mommy's tummy. "Bobby's mommy got really big before his brother was born. Mommy," he plowed on, "you don't look any bigger."

"Thank you, I think," Sandra said with a laugh. "Michael, we are going to adopt your baby sister," she said. "Another mommy got big in her tummy and had a baby girl. That mommy is not able to keep her, she is giving her baby girl to us so we can love and care for her."

"What's her name?" Michael asked puzzled.

"She doesn't have one yet. We will name her when she comes home."

"How come she doesn't have a name? That's weird."

Even though Sandra and Jay assumed that the baby had a name on her birth certificate, they did not want to confuse Michael any further. Sandra tried to simplify the issue, "She is called baby girl and she's so little that she doesn't really know. We are going to give her a beautiful name and a wonderful home."

"I don't know," Michael thought out loud, "I would be really mad if I didn't have a name. How would my teacher call on me? I wouldn't answer to baby boy. That's just embarrassing."

"Don't worry, Michael. She'll be fine," comforted Jay.

"When is she coming here?"

"Soon."

"How soon?"

"She's in a special home called a foster home until she is eating and sleeping well enough to come to us," Jay said.

"Is there something wrong with her?"

"No Michael. She is perfectly fine," Jay emphasized.

"This is weird. How come her mommy and daddy don't want her? Was she bad?"

"No Michael. She is very good. Her mommy and daddy felt they could not take care of her like we will," reassured Sandra as she gave him a hug.

"I don't know about this. Why did you pick a girl? I think I would have more fun with a brother."

"Michael, we have an amazing son. We thought it would be really nice to have a daughter. She will be lots of fun. You will see," Sandra said.

"Let's talk about this more tomorrow. It's time for our big seven year old to get some sleep," said Jay. "Good night son."

He and Sandra kissed Michael and then Sandra tucked him in and whispered, "You will like her Michael. It's going to be wonderful having her here."

Michael was not so sure. He would much rather a brother. What was he going to do with a silly sister? "Goodnight Mommy."

"Goodnight Michael," Sandra said, "We love you."

Sandra and Jay headed to their room. "Michael had more questions than I expected," Jay said as he pulled his shirt over his head. "I hadn't given the notion of the baby not officially having her new name much thought."

"Children do come up with the craziest things," replied Sandra. "I was surprised that he knew to look at my belly. I didn't think he would make that connection. I guess he and his friends did notice Bobby's mother grow bigger during her pregnancy with David."

"I guess so. Tell me again what the last foster care report said."

"The report was not very detailed, but the caseworker told me that the baby is growing each week and is eating better. Her sleep pattern is also improving. I don't know for sure if they need her to do something before she gets to come home or if a certain number of weeks need to go by for the waiting period. I think it just needs to be three full months."

"I think you're right. We're almost there," Jay reassured her as he pulled her close. They swayed together for a few moments. Minutes later, as they settled into bed for the night, Jay asked, "Do you know anything about the foster care parents? Do you know how many children are grouped in foster care households?"

"Not really. I could ask Barbara if she knows," Sandra replied. "Mrs. Berman did say that they had used the particular foster home before and that the baby would be fine."

"That is good, but maybe you should ask Barbara. I'm sure the foster parents are wonderful people and know what they are doing," Jay trailed off trying to convince himself as well as Sandra. With images of a baby girl crying unnoticed by her harried, overextended foster parents, Jay fell into a troubled sleep.

***

Two weeks later, cancer scored another victory. Grandpa Jules succumbed suddenly. He had caught a fever and things progressed downhill from there. He was laid to rest on a bitter, cold day in mid-February. With a high of 25 degrees, the temperature had dropped significantly from the day before and the family stood huddled together at the gravesite chilled by both the tragedy and the punishing winds.

"Oh, Jay," Sandra sobbed leaning into his arm which was wrapped around her shoulders, "this is truly the saddest day! We will all miss Grandpa Jules so very much!"

Sobbing as well, Jay pulled her closer. With difficulty, he recited the traditional Jewish mourning prayer led by the rabbi.

Chapter Fourteen

Friday, April 19, 1963

Two long months had passed. The pivotal day had arrived. Jay and Sandra dressed carefully for the appointment at the Jewish Adoption Center. This was the day they would meet their daughter and bring her home.

"I'm excited and worried," Sandra said checking her cherry-red lipstick in the mirror over the bureau. "This is so different than the day Michael was born," she continued while smoothing down her pretty yet modest mint green and navy dress.

"I know what you mean," Jay agreed gazing into the same mirror to catch Sandra's eye. "We loved Michael from the moment he was conceived and the love grew unconditionally as he grew within you," he said, adjusting his fashionable thin beige and gray tie.

"I know that we truly want this baby and that we will love her, but it is different," Sandra completed the thought.

"We will grow to love her. It may not be instantaneous," Jay said pulling Sandra into his arms for a hug of support. "She will be wonderful. I know it." Jay smiled encouragingly.

"Of course she will. And Michael will take to her right away," Sandra chimed with promise as she carefully rolled on white, elbow length gloves.

"Yes. Indeed he will," he said as he pulled on his charcoal suit jacket. "It's time to go. Are you ready?" Jay asked.

"Yes. I think so," was Sandra's reply as she placed a navy hat upon her head. The hat, she reflected, had a dual purpose; it completed her ensemble and when pulled low would partially cover her face and hide her personage upon entering the office. Although she had made great progress, Sandra did have some residual feelings of embarrassment about her infertility and the need to go this route.

Jay drove the ten minute drive to the Jewish Adoption Center, and they arrived right on time. As they walked up the path, they made a striking pair unknowingly undoing Sandra's precautionary hat trick. Once inside, the adoption formalities included detailed paperwork that was signed and witnessed before they were able to see the baby. Nervous and excited, Jay and Sandra attended to the instructions given by Mrs. Berman, although afterward they realized how inattentive they had truly been. It did sink in that there was a one-year period during which Mrs. Berman would make home visits to check on the baby and during which time they had the option of returning the baby to the agency if there were problems at home. The idea was both comforting and frightening revealed by the mixed emotions evident on their faces as they nodded their heads in understanding.

Finally, Mrs. Berman left the room to get the baby. Sandra reached for Jay's hand as they both stared at the open doorway. A moment of pure wonderment ensued when Mrs. Berman returned and placed their beautiful baby girl in Sandra's welcoming arms. Tears appeared in all the adult eyes as they looked down upon the newest member of the Brenner family. Big bright full-awake dark chocolate brown eyes looked up into the face of her new mother. Squirming a bit at the unfamiliar embrace, the baby blinked a few times and then she smiled.

"I think she's smiling!" Jay exclaimed.

"She is simply beautiful," breathed Sandra as she kissed the baby's head for the first time.

"Yes she is. Extraordinary!" Jay concurred emphatically.

"All is in order. Congratulations Mr. and Mrs. Brenner. May she bring you much joy," Mrs. Berman pronounced as she brushed a stray tear aside. This was the true satisfaction of her job and the moments that made it bearable. As she continued to look at Sandra Brenner's happy face the image merged with the tear-stricken devastated face of young Jo Engle wishing the same baby farewell. Shaking her head to clear the conflicting images, Mrs. Berman directed the Brenner family to the door. "Good luck to you. I will be by next week to see how you are faring. Good day." She closed the door and sighed heavily as she wiped her eyes with a handkerchief handily pulled from her sleeve.

At the door, Jay and Sandra removed the serviceable white blanket in which the baby was bundled and carefully wrapped her in a warm pink blanket they had brought for her. Having removed the outward vestiges of the baby's former life, Jay and Sandra made their way to the car with their new daughter. Juggling the baby in one arm as she pulled her hat lower on her face, Sandra looked around and gratefully saw no one. She cradled the three month old tightly in her arms as Jay drove them home.

"She seems to have a nice temperament," Sandra said quietly. "She is still wide awake."

Jay glanced across at the baby and smiled, "She seems very content with you, Sandra."

"Yes. So far so good. Do you think everyone will have arrived?"

"The family is very excited. I'm sure some of them are waiting to meet her. The rest will probably be over later in the week."

"How did Michael seem to you this morning?"

"He appeared fine. I think he's ready."

"I hope so."

As they turned into the alley behind their house, they saw Michael waiting in the kitchen by the back door. His nose was pressed up against the glass panel. Condensation made an imprint of his nose on the glass.

Jay and Sandra pulled in behind the garage, and then Jay helped Sandra alight from the car while still holding the baby. He brushed the baby's cheek as they walked the short distance to the back door while Michael ran to meet them.

"Hey Michael," Jay exclaimed as he swooped Michael up in his arms. "Here is your new sister, Ellen," Jay said positioning Michael in front of the new baby.

"You weren't able to get a boy after all," Michael said clearly disappointed.

"No Michael. She is a girl." Jay and Sandra looked toward each other and Sandra shook her head. "Remember we told you that the baby was definitely a girl," Jay responded.

93

"I know. I was just hoping," Michael conceded as he looked into his sister's face.

"Isn't she pretty, Michael?" Sandra suggested.

"Yeah. She's okay," Michael replied.

"Let's get everyone inside. It's too cool out here for the baby," Jay said as he led Michael toward the door. Sandra followed with Ellen.

They made their way inside and headed toward the dining room. Jay put Michael down.

"The baby is here!" yelled Michael.

Startled by the loud noise, baby Ellen began to cry. Sandra and Jay looked at each other. "Here we go," laughed Jay.

Jay's mother, Grandma Rena, and her sister Aunt Bertha came forward to take a peek. Grandma Rena was choked up with emotion. "Oh my Jules would have been so proud. He would have cherished her," she said as she dabbed at her eyes and wiped away bittersweet tears. "I miss him so," she said as Jay reached over to comfort her.

He pulled her close and then said for all to hear, "We have named her Ellen Jo, Mom. She will carry on the family tradition." It was a tradition that the middle name of each male member of the Brenner family was Jay. Jay's full name was Justin Jay and Jules was Julian Jay and so on through the recent generations. However, Michael was the exception, because Sandra's father had died shortly before Michael's birth. In Sandra's father's merit and by Jewish tradition, Jay and Sandra had chosen to honor Sandra's father by giving Michael the name Michael Lawrence, the same first and middle name as Sandra's father. With Jules's passing just two months previously, Jay and Sandra had decided to name their new baby girl after him, Jo for Jay, a female rendition. Jay hugged his mother tightly as mother and son gazed at the infant with a shared understanding.

Next to welcome the baby was Grandma Lil guided by her sisters, Aunt Shirley and Aunt Hannah. They directed her hand toward the baby and Grandma Lil stroked her cheek. The ladies murmured in approval and the soft touch of her grandmother soothed the baby as she looked around at all the smiling faces. "She is smiling, Lil. She has a good head of brown hair and beautiful bright brown eyes. She's so precious, what a lovely girl!" exclaimed Aunt Shirley. "Hershel will be along right after the dinner hour at the business. I can't wait for him to see Ellen. He will be so thrilled by her!"

The ladies took turns holding baby Ellen as well as entertaining her big brother who was none too pleased with sharing the attention. As the ladies inundated Sandra with advice, Jay begged off and headed to the office for the afternoon. He promised to return for an early dinner. Eventually Ellen cried, and it was determined by the group that she was hungry. Sandra fed her and then put her down for her first nap in her new home.

Once Grandma Rena and all the aunts had left trailing hugs and kisses for the new family addition and her brother, the house grew quiet. Only Sandra, Michael, Ellen and Grandma Lil remained.

"She doesn't do very much, does she Mommy?" Michael questioned.

"Not yet, but she is very small, Michael. She will start to do things before long."

"But you said she would be fun."

"And she will," Sandra said brushing his close-cropped wavy brown hair back on his forehead. "In time, she will start to do things just like Bobby's brother, David. It took a while but now he is crawling around and you have fun with him. Give her some time, Michael. Would you like to watch some television? I think the Flintstones is on channel 11 in a few minutes."

"Yabba Dabba Doo!"

"Wonderful," laughed Sandra. "Mother do you think you could sit with Michael while he watches? I would love to lie down for a few minutes while the baby is sleeping."

"Of course, Sandra. Go ahead. I'm sure you are tired. Michael will be fine with me."

The three traipsed down to the basement. Michael's playroom was a small area of the basement. It was a dark paneled room with a patterned area rug and beige sofa set away from the stairwell. A small black and white television sat on a low table. Michael pulled Grandma Lil toward the sofa as Sandra set the television station.

"Thanks Mother. Be good Michael," she said on her way upstairs.

Yawning, Sandra headed up to her bedroom. What a day this has been, she thought as she glanced toward the closed door where her new daughter was sleeping. We have a daughter, she thought with pride. Hopefully I can get a half hour of rest and get dinner started before she wakes up.

Chapter Fifteen

April 1963

Jo and Carol flopped into their seats in the spacious Monument Theatre, a Baltimore landmark movie house decorated in the Art Deco style with seating for over 1000. The decision to go was a last minute one, and they laughed at the comical mad dash that had miraculously landed them there with minutes to spare. The day's feature was the newly released film *Bye Bye Birdie*. The movie musical was purported to be funny and entertaining by the newspaper reviews and with the comical Dick Van Dyke and gorgeous Janet Leigh heading the cast, it couldn't miss. Glancing past Carol toward the entrance, Jo noticed a striking young man stylishly attired in a snazzy yellow sweater vest over a crisp white shirt pulled together with finely pressed brown pants.

Jo leaned toward Carol and whispered, "Who is that boy by the door?"

Following Jo's gaze, Carol answered, "I think he's a friend of Ross. I believe I met him at Joe's party a few weeks ago."

"Hmmm. Do you remember his name?"

"Let me see. I think… George. Can't remember his last name," Carol whispered back. "He is kind of cute."

"Yes, he is. Oh. I see Ross coming in just now. Good. Maybe he'll introduce us after the show."

"The lights are going down. I'm glad we came!" Carol exclaimed smoothing the collar of her new raspberry cardigan.

"Me too."

Many laughs later, the curtain went down and the lights went up. Humming and smiling, the girls made their way toward the exit. It was a sunny early spring day and the girls shielded their eyes as they headed out of the theater. George stepped outside just behind Jo and bumped into her.

"I'm so sorry. The sun blinded me for a moment," he explained apologetically.

"That's okay. It's very bright out," Jo replied sweetly, just as Ross joined the small group on the pavement.

"Do you know each other?" Ross asked.

"Unfortunately no. I accidentally bumped into this very lovely girl as I was coming out into the sunlight," George said indicating Jo.

"George Millstein, this is Jo Engle and Carol Rosen. Jo, George," Ross introduced.

"So nice to meet you, George," Jo smiled as she took in his above average height, lanky build, thick chestnut hair and intense brown eyes.

"It's certainly my pleasure," George answered with a grin, stretching out the word certainly flirtatiously.

Carol glanced at Jo and noticed a glimmer in her eye. Uh, oh, thought Carol. Ross is foiled again.

***

Jo had successfully begun to move on. Three months had passed since the birth and there was just one formality left to do. Jo needed to officially turn over custody of the baby to the Jewish Adoption Center. As Mrs. Berman drove Jo to the district courthouse, Jo gushed, "I really like being a secretary at a publishing company. I love to read and it's fun to be a part of it all. And things are much better at home now that Mitchell and Agnes have stopped yelling about my pregnancy. We go out a lot," Jo trailed off thinking about George, but she did not dare share any information about her new boyfriend with Mrs. Berman, because she was afraid the caseworker would lecture her on promiscuous behavior. The ride was pleasant and Jo continued to be upbeat.

The formality at the courthouse was quickly accomplished. Jo appeared before the court judge and agreed in a clear voice to the transfer of custody. Time had helped her deal with the loss to some degree even though she certainly still had moments of doubt and sadness, but she was rebuilding her life and it was going well.

As they said their final goodbyes in the idling car outside Aunt Bessie and Uncle Henry's house, Mrs. Berman said, "You seem to be doing remarkably well, Jo. I am very pleased. Please send my best wishes to your aunt and uncle."

In direct contrast to the summer before, Jo enjoyed the freedom and hope of a single, coming of age, young woman as the summer of 1963 arrived. Her relationship with George was advancing steadily and she considered re-enrolling in college for the fall semester. Tamping down sporadic conflicting emotions and concerns about Louisa, she didn't allow her thoughts about the baby to interfere with her happiness.   Her future appeared as bright and beautiful as the weather on that Independence Day.

As she readied herself to spend the holiday with George, she dressed festively in a delicate cotton blue dress with a red and white scarf. The dainty silver heart earrings that George had given her the month before dangled from her ears and completed her ensemble.   "Will you be back by 4:30 for the barbeque?" Aunt Bessie called from the kitchen as Jo passed on her way to the front door.

"Of course. Should I come back early to help?" Jo asked through the kitchen doorway.

"No, dear. Enjoy yourself with George. Bring him along if you want."

"Thank you, Aunt Bessie. I think I will."

Smiling, she waved goodbye to her Aunt Bessie as she skipped out the door.

Jo and George watched the parade pass by on Reeve Street. A large crowd lined both sides. Holding tightly to George's hand, the couple found a spot. Huddled close together, they laughed often as they enjoyed the music and costumes of the school bands and the antics of the clowns. Street vendors sold drinks and treats, and George bought a huge lemonade for them to share. Giggling, they put two straws in and drank the whole thing down.

"My lips are all puckered. It was so tart," Jo said as she smacked her lips together and then apart.

"Is that so? Let me feel," George said as he leaned in for a bold kiss.

"George," Jo scolded, "not in public! What will people think?"

"I don't really care. You taste delicious."

"Let's go down to the harbor and walk. Maybe there won't be so many people there."

"And why do you want to go someplace with less people?"

"You will see," she said as she pulled him along.

At 4:30 promptly, Jo and George arrived at Edge Road. As they walked around back, family friends were assembled for the barbeque. Red, white and blue streamers decorated the serving table and the paper goods were also in theme. Incongruously with the spirit of the day, everyone seemed rather serious although animated as they approached.

Reaching Uncle Henry by the grill, Jo asked him, "Has something bad happened?"

"Oh no. Something historic is happening!" he replied with gusto. "Bessie was just watching television as she shucked the corn and she heard the most amazing thing. Over 300 people descended on Liberty Hill Park in an organized anti-segregation march. The marchers organized themselves and were led by many clergymen from all faiths including a few well known rabbis from the community."

"Wow!" Jo and George exclaimed at the same time.

"The newscaster said that once the marchers reached the park, the police were there in force and the police chief read them the Maryland Trespass Act and began arresting all the marchers and taking them to the police station. This is still happening as we speak."

"Why Liberty Hill Park?" asked George.

"Because they have a 'whites only' policy," replied Uncle Henry.

"Do you think the march will persuade them to change it?"

"I don't know. But if enough people stop going there, it may force them to in order to stay in business."

"Come inside quickly!" Bessie yelled from the doorway. "There's a broadcast of the marchers singing 'We Shall Overcome' – come quick."

Everyone piled inside, the barbeque temporarily forgotten. Uncle Henry totally forgot the hamburgers he was cooking. When he returned a half hour later, they were completely charred. A small price for watching history, he chuckled to himself as he threw them in the trash can.

After the delayed barbeque, George and Jo finished their memorable day at the famous Memorial Stadium watching the Orioles beat the Los Angeles Angels by the score of 7-4. "I love you, Jo," George murmured in her ear as red, white and blue Fourth of July fireworks lit the sky of the infield. The popping explosions added to Jo's happiness as her heart experienced tiny fireworks of its own.

"I love you too, George. I'm so happy. Thank you for such an amazing day!" Jo replied as she turned to peck him on the cheek quickly snuggling in close. This has been one of the best days of my life, Jo thought. She was amazed how bright her future seemed once again.

That night in her room, with her heart overflowing, she pulled out and kissed a small picture from her wallet, a picture she stored in her purse and carried with her always. Nurse Stephens had thoughtfully given her the black and white photo as she was leaving the hospital. "I miss you my darling Louisa, but I know you are being well cared for. I hope you're as happy as I am," Jo whispered.

***

1963 was a pivotal year in Jo's life and it was certainly a pivotal year in the history of the United States. As the country mourned the assassination of President John F. Kennedy, Jo woke on the morning of the funeral November 25 and quickly rushed to the bathroom. Nausea had set in and she recognized the pattern. She sat down on the bathroom floor, feeling the cold tiles through her thin nightgown exacerbated by the cold fear that crept through her. Frantically, she thought, how could I have let this happen again? She heard the phone ringing downstairs and her aunt's pleasant voice in response. Shivering, she pulled herself up and made her way back to the bedroom as Aunt Bessie called, "Jo, George is on the line for you."

Reaching for her robe at the end of the bed and the Kleenex box beside it, she called back, "I'll be right there." She pulled on her robe and turned quickly smacking her elbow on the open door handle. Miserably, she rubbed her stinging elbow as she quickly making her way down the stairs to the phone in the living room. "Thank you Aunt Bessie," she said breathlessly as she retrieved the phone from her aunt, but not before Bessie noticed how disheveled and wretched she looked.

"Everything okay, dear?" Aunt Bessie inquired, eyebrows raised.

"I got up quickly and banged my elbow."

Perceiving more than Jo's response indicated, Aunt Bessie stated, "Please come see me after you have spoken to George."

"Ok," Jo answered unhappily. She wasn't ready to share with her aunt just yet, but she knew that Aunt Bessie would get the information from her in short order.

"Hi George," Jo sighed plopping down on the stool by the phone and pulling at the long phone cord.

"Hi Jo. I'm headed to work but I just wanted to check and see what you wanted to do tonight. I think some of the kids are getting together at Joe's to watch the President's funeral on the news at six and the special report at seven."

"That's fine. I get off at five. I'll be ready," she said formally.

"Is everything ok? You sound a bit stiff."

"I am frazzled. Running late. I'm sorry George. I'll see you later."

"Ok, honey. I'll see you later. I love you."

"Really?"

"Of course. Is there some reason not to love you?" he asked playfully.

"No, no of course not. I love you too, George," Jo answered sadly.

She quickly ran back up the stairs to her room and finished getting dressed. Thankfully the nausea was subsiding, so she focused on George's words of love. Jo thought back to her time with Lenny. The differences in the two relationships were clearly evident. The secretive element with Lenny had seemed exciting, but she now knew that it had been a cover. She had thought the whole professor-student thing was the entire reason for the big secret, but his married status had been. George was not Lenny. She had met his family and his friends, often on double-dates. Same predicament, different relationship, she thought furrowing her brow. She would tell George and surely he would do the right thing. She clung to that thought – grasping – hoping that it would be true.

Jo found Aunt Bessie in the kitchen.

"I'm sorry, Aunt Bessie. I don't want to be late for work. Could we speak later? I really am fine."

"All right, Jo. You looked a bit off. I saw something in your face, but now you do seem fine. I suppose the President's death has upset us all. Do you want some breakfast?"

"No, thank you. I'm not hungry."

"Make sure to eat later. Have a good day, dear."

It was a profoundly sad day for the country, and it seemed that everyone was mourning. Jo's sad, disillusioned expression reflected in the eyes of each person she encountered. At the gathering with George and their friends that evening, the girls sobbed openly, as they watched the television coverage of the tremendously poised Jacqueline Kennedy along with Caroline and little John Jr. bravely marching behind the casket of their husband and father. Jo clung to George. As she cried, he pulled her close comforting her.

The nausea pattern continued, so Jo made an appointment with Dr. Goodman. She called in sick to work and made her way to Dr. Goodman's office alone, too embarrassed to even call Carol this time.

The same disapproving nurse from her first visit to the office led her back to the examination room, mumbling about stupid young girls and shaking her head repeatedly. Sadly, Jo realized that her truthfulness when she made the appointment and told the receptionist the reason for her visit had been relayed to the judgmental nurse leading her. What they must think of me, Jo thought.

Dr. Goodman was as caring and nice as previously, although his expression was sad. "I will call you in two weeks' time with the results, Miss Engle," he said once again.

"Would it be okay if I call you at a certain time of the day?" Jo asked hesitantly, "I am living at my aunt and uncle's home and my aunt may answer the phone."

"I do all my calls at the end of the day, but I will be certain that I ask for you directly and only share the results with you."

"Thank you doctor," Jo answered letting out a breath she hadn't realized she was holding.

"I would suggest, young lady, that you prepare yourself and possibly your aunt and uncle as well." He paused and then quietly asked, "Is the same young man responsible?"

"No. It is different now, I hope. I have much to do."

"Good luck to you, Miss Engle. Good luck."

***

Crunch went the glass under George's feet, the symbol of the holy temple and the reminder that the Jewish people won't ever forget its destruction. Jo and George stood before a small audience in Rabbi

Greenfield's study in Richmond, Virginia. "Well, Mrs. Millstein," George said as he kissed Jo, "how is my beautiful bride?"

"I am happy, Mr. Millstein," she answered with a big smile.

"How's the nausea?"

"Much better now. I should be able to eat some lunch."

"Good. I am hungry and I'm sure the baby is hungry too."

George's parents, Aunt Bessie and Uncle Henry were the only other people in attendance at the December wedding of Jo and George Millstein. The decision to have Rabbi Greenfield officiate was due to the need for an expedited service, prompted by a confirmed pregnancy and extremely distressed parents and guardians, combined with a no-waiting period necessary marriage rule in Virginia. After thanking Rabbi Greenfield, the small group made their way to a quaint Colonial style restaurant close to the rabbi's study and had a festive lunch. At least the young couple found it festive. The adults were subdued; each saddened by the speedy result of reckless young behavior, but satisfied that the situation had been dealt with.

"We are glad you have each other," Aunt Bessie said as she kissed Jo goodbye.

"Indeed. We hope you will be very happy," Uncle Henry added.

"Thank you both. Thank you for sharing our day with us. It means a lot to me," Jo said hugging her aunt and uncle.

After honeymooning in Virginia for two days, the young couple returned to live with George's parents. Pregnancy number two was progressing, and Jo would start to show any day. While sitting on their bed in the small bedroom provided by her in-laws, she twisted the simple gold band on her ring finger. This baby she would keep. Life was good, she thought. She pulled out the small picture from her wallet and kissed the tiny face for the hundredth time. "I hope you're as happy as I am," she whispered.

Chapter Sixteen

January 1964

Baby Ellen was a year old, and the family gathered to celebrate. Ellen teetered about the house decked out in her first pair of shoes, a special gift from Aunt Shirley and Uncle Hershel.

Uncle Hershel believed that special care must be taken when buying shoes. "The feet must be well cared for, so they will take us where we need to go," he often said.

"Lil," Aunt Shirley touched her sister on the arm, "Ellen is adorable. Her new shoes are snow white patent leather Mary Janes and she is almost running in them. She will be pulling you along in no time. Her brunette hair is getting thicker and she looks wonderful in the pink dress you bought for her."

"Thank you, Shirley," replied Grandma Lil, "thank you for taking me to get it for her."

"Hershel and I were pleased to do it. You know how much we love Ellen."

"Yes, I do Shirley. You already spoil her."

"Babies can't be spoiled. Here comes Sandra with the cake."

It was a smaller group for this birthday celebration, Grandma Rena with her two sisters and Grandma Lil with Hannah, Shirley and Hershel. Jay scooped up Ellen who was toddling by as Michael rushed past bee-lining his way to the cake just as Sandra placed it on the table.

"I'll blow out the candles. Ellen is too little!" He exclaimed.

"You can help her after we sing," replied Sandra helplessly as Michael blew with all his strength and caused the two candles, one for the first birthday and one for the future, to topple over into the cake. One was still flickering and Sandra quickly pressed it into the cake to smother the flame.

Immediately, Ellen reacted to the disturbance and started to cry, so Jay held her more tightly and soothed her with kisses and hushed words of love. With teary eyes, Ellen listened as they sang "Happy Birthday" to her. After Michael had been chastised by Jay for his exuberance, cake was enjoyed by all, and especially by the birthday girl who made a huge mess of it smearing it all over the table of her high chair.

Later that night, a tradition was started. Jay and Sandra had discussed the best way to tell Ellen that she was adopted. They decided on a bedtime story. Each night they told Ellen the following story:

Once upon a time, there was a very special baby. She was adorable with big, brown eyes and brown hair and everyone loved her. What made this baby extra special was that she was adopted. The mommy who had the baby grow in her belly was not able to take care of her, so she gave the baby to a mommy and daddy that wanted her very much and could take good care of her. The mommy and daddy and her new big brother were so happy that they danced and laughed and tickled the baby – you!

With rapt attention, Ellen listened to the story, although they found she much preferred dancing to being tickled.

The next week, Barbara Greene stopped by for a visit.

"Sandra, I brought a little outfit for Ellen. I couldn't resist once I saw it."

"Thank you, Barbara, you are a dear. It's charming," Sandra said as she pulled the pink two piece laced-edged jumper and shirt set from the box Barbara had handed her.

"Can I get you tea or coffee? Please tell me you can visit for a bit. I would love a few minutes of adult talk. I have almost forgotten what conversation with another adult feels like. Life is so much busier with a baby."

"I remember the endless bottles and diapers and the lack of sleep. I came by, because I wanted to catch up with you and see how things are really going. I have some time before the kids come home from school and yes, I would love a cup of coffee."

"Coming right up. Let me get it started and I'll be right back," Sandra said as she went into the kitchen.

"Well?" Barbara inquired once Sandra was back and settled in the seat at the dining room table beside her.

"Things are good. Ellen is a sweet baby and had a fine report from Dr. Jones, her pediatrician. She has hit all the milestones, eats well, sleeps through and is growing steadily."

"Wonderful. How is Michael doing with her?"

"Fine, I guess. He is anxious for her to be able to do more. As you know, he's a spirited seven year old boy. Sometimes he is really helpful with her, but more often he tries to take her toys away from her and get a rise out of her. Boys will be boys – so they say," Sandra said with a small smile.

"Does he ever say anything about her being adopted?"

"No, not really anymore. He did for the first few months. He kept asking if she was staying, but we told him she was our daughter and his sister and will always be a part of our family. Of course we didn't tell him that there really is a clause in the adoption agreement for up to a year that allows us to relinquish the baby if there are problems at home and the arrangement is not working."

"That is a jolting thought, but I can imagine that there are times when the fit is not right. I'm so glad that you and Jay have found the perfect fit and now have a beautiful daughter to fill out your family."

"We have you to thank, Barbara. I'm not sure we would've ever thought to try without you and your encouragement," Sandra said as she embraced Barbara. You are a great friend to us, you and Bernard. We are amazingly lucky to have you. Oh, the coffee smells ready. I'll be right back."

"Thanks for the coffee, it is delicious," Barbara said, once Sandra returned with two steaming cups. "Have you and Jay thought about what you will tell Ellen about her birth?"

"We actually did somewhat. We made up a bedtime story that explains about adoption. We say that another mommy had her and gave her to us to care for because she could not. We started telling her the story on her birthday. By telling her the story repeatedly, we hope to get her to know about it but not be scared or surprised about it all of a sudden when she's older. We really don't want this to be a big thing. We just need her to know."

"The bedtime story is an interesting idea. Did you read about it or did someone suggest you do this?"

"Dr. Jones suggested it. He's a brilliant pediatrician."

Sandra and Jay made sure they told Ellen the story with frequency until Ellen understood the story and could repeat it along with them. More importantly, they continued until they felt that Ellen understood what it meant to be adopted.

***

"Ellen, can you tell me the story about when you were born?" Jay asked as he hugged her close. Jay and Ellen were sitting on Ellen's big girl bed in her newly decorated red and white room. White curtains with tiny red rosebuds draped the three windows in her corner room. Jay glanced at the carpeting distracted by his color blindness and curious as to what color the carpeting actually was.

Before three-year old Ellen could answer he asked, "Ellen, what color is the carpeting?"

"It's red red Daddy," Ellen answered crinkling up her nose in distaste.

Having confirmed his feeling that the color was very bold, Jay shook his head. He had a brutal headache. As he pressed his hand against his head, Ellen asked, "Daddy, did you hurt yourself?"

"No honey, but my head does hurt – I guess I have hurt myself a little," he chuckled.

"Let me kiss it and make it better." Ellen leaned over and gave him a warm kiss on his forehead.

"Thank you so much. I do feel better."

Ellen smiled and moved even closer. "Daddy, I know the story. I can tell it to you today," Ellen offered sweetly.

"That's a great idea."

"There was once a pretty little baby – me- and I grew in a mommy's belly. That mommy could not take good care of me, so she gave me to you and Mommy to take care of me and love me. I love you Daddy. I'm glad you got me from the other mommy."

"I'm so glad we did too, Ellen. Do you know what it is called – the big word?"

Without hesitation, Ellen answered, "Adopted. I was adopted."

"Wonderful Ellen. I think you do understand now," he said giving her a hug and kiss. "Let's read a book. How about 'The Three Billy Goats Gruff?'"

"Make the funny sounds this time. Please Daddy."

After much neighing and laughing, Jay tucked Ellen in bed making sure she had her favorite stuffed bunny. He kissed her goodnight. "Sleep well, my little love."

"Sandra," Jay said upon finding Sandra cleaning up the last few things from dinner in the kitchen, "Ellen understands. I think it is finally time to stop with the story."

"That's wonderful news. Dr. Jones said she should be able to understand around three."

From that moment on, the topic was no longer discussed. They had decided to make the adoption a non-issue.

Chapter Seventeen

February 1968

It was a rare evening indeed for Sandra and Jay. Sandra's mother and Ellen were visiting and staying the night with Uncle Hershel and Aunt Shirley, while Michael enjoyed a sleepover at his friend Larry's. Alone in the house for the first time in years, they relaxed on the sofa in the living room. Jay's long left arm enveloped Sandra and kept her close. With his right hand, he sipped a gin and tonic from his favorite short, rounded glass known by the family as the "rollie pollie". Sandra sipped on sherry sighing in contentment.

"It's wonderful to have some time alone," she said.

"Yes, it certainly is," his deep voice was a low rumble in Sandra's ear as she leaned her head on his chest.

Quietly she asked, "Do you think Michael is behaving?"

"I think Doris has her hands full, but it will be okay. He spends enough time over there for Doris to know what to do to keep him in line."

"He and Larry make such a pair."

"Yes, that's the truth."

"I think Ellen is doing well."

"Of course. Why wouldn't she? Shirley and Hershel dote on her. She will be spoiled tonight."

"Jay, I don't mean tonight. I mean in general," Sandra said sitting up to face Jay. "Do you think she is in any way different, because of the adoption? Do you see her developing any strange traits?"

"No, not at all. What has prompted this?"

"Jim and Carla at your office party last week."

"Sandra," Jay began disturbed by the turn of the conversation, "they adopted an older child with physical issues. They think he may have been mistreated at a foster home and is having a hard time adjusting."

"That must be so difficult for them."

"Jim and Carla are amazing people with so much love to give. They knew there would be challenges, sometimes Carla talks about it too much. You caught her after a tough day. Usually she is all smiles about Jim, Jr."

"I see," she paused and considered then added, "but Ellen is so sensitive. She gets upset easily it seems to me. Do you think her mother was that way as well?"

"Sandra, you are her mother. She doesn't have another one. She gets upset often because Michael picks on her constantly, and she is young and hasn't figured out how to get him to stop or fight back."

"Don't blame it all on Michael. He didn't ask for a sister and I think he isn't so enamored with the idea."

"Michael likes Ellen just fine. He's being an eleven year-old boy and eleven-year old boys pick on their sisters and find their sisters annoying."

"Danny was never like that with me. He followed me around and was very gentle."

"Sandra, your brother was younger than you and he idolized you. It is not the same at all."

"Jay," Sandra chose another tack, "do you think we did the right thing?"

"Sandra, what are you trying to say? Are you unhappy with Ellen as your daughter?"

"No, I don't mean that at all. Sandra debated before asking, "Do you love her like you love Michael?"

"Yes, I do," he replied after a steadying breath. "I love her with all my heart. She is different than Michael, but I do love her unconditionally as if she was my flesh and blood."

"I love her too Jay, I really do," Sandra said with tears brimming. "But I have to be honest. It is different."

Bright sun, warm sand, a dazzling smile that rivaled the sparkles off the gentle waves, he almost felt the day anew. A cherished memory of Ellen, building sandcastles with deliberate care, tongue peeking out between her teeth as she concentrated on getting the edges smooth and neat. Dressed in a two piece striped concoction with a big flower on the backside, he remembered laughing as she bent over to fill her bucket with water at the ocean's edge. He saw her in his mind's eye, trudging back up to the spot beside his chair, looking up to make sure he was there and then flashing a smile filled with pure love, his heart melting. Sandra had been there as well, head buried in a book oblivious to the goings on. More involved with Ellen's welfare on a day-to-day basis, Sandra happily relinquished Ellen's care to Jay during the yearly beach trips to Ocean City. In truth, she did not have the patience or desire to play with Ellen as she once had with Michael. Perhaps it was the seven year difference in age. Perhaps it was the difference in relationship. Loving an adopted child the same as your own is not a given, he thought.

"It is wonderful that you love her and take such care of her Sandra. You should be proud of that. You are a great mother to her – the only one she has. We did the right thing, I know we did," he said.

"Of course you're right. I just needed to hear it," she said. It would be nice to be so sure, she thought.

"Let's go out to eat," Jay prompted a change of plans. "We still have the entire night to be home alone. How about Italian?"

"That sounds perfect," Sandra replied somewhat comforted by Jay's expression of unequivocal conviction, and not wanting to ruin the evening, she gladly dropped the subject.

Chapter Eighteen

May 1970

"Maybe she's a famous ballerina!" Linda exclaimed as she turned and looked at Ellen. Ellen and three of her closest friends sat lined up on a group of swings on the playground of their elementary school during recess, the tips of their shoes dug into the sand that filled the play area.

"I bet she's really pretty," Julie chimed in.

"I do too," Ellen concurred, "but if she is so famous then she would have money to hire people to watch me when she's dancing."

"Maybe she just got famous," Linda suggested. "She wasn't rich when you were born, so she had to put you up for adoption."

"Then, she might want me back," Ellen said excitedly as she imagined the scenario and found it both scary and thrilling.

"She might," Linda encouraged.

"I think she's a famous singer instead," Debbie insisted.

"Why a singer and not a ballerina?" Linda asked.

"Because Ellen has a pretty voice," Debbie replied.

"Oh," said Ellen, "that's nice, Debbie. I like that."

Ellen was seven years old. It was recess time and she and her friends were on the playground of Dale

Elementary School. The girls were the best of friends. They all lived in what was known as "The Village", a residential area with small colonial style comfortable houses located behind the school. Ellen lived on the farthest street. When she walked to school, she stopped and picked up her friends on the way. It was a fun way to walk to school each day. The girls' conversation had gravitated back to one of their favorite topics, Ellen's adoption and the mystery of her birth mother. They enjoyed imagining and guessing the kind of person Ellen's biological mother could have been and were intrigued with the idea that Ellen had another mother somewhere that she had not met nor may ever meet her. The topic also fascinated Ellen, but her fascination was a mixture of desire to know her mother, angst about finding the true circumstances of her adoption, curiosity about where she came from and fear of finding out hurtful things.

Just as quickly as it was brought up, the girls dropped the subject and ran off to the monkey bars to climb.

Later that day, Ellen was home working on her homework at the dining room table when Michael passed by. He was in the ninth grade, his last year of junior high school, and he disapproved of Ellen's studiousness. He was not a particularly gifted student, and it irked him immensely to see Ellen succeed at her studies while he struggled so with his.

"What are you doing, Ellen?" he asked as he tossed a tennis ball up and down in the air.

"My math homework," she answered and returned to her math problems.

"Why are you doing your homework? You don't need to do that." He insisted as he pulled at her paper.

"Don't do that, you'll rip it!"

"You are such a baby, stop crying," he said as he let go of the paper. He had made a big tear across the bottom and Ellen became upset. She looked up at him with tears in her eyes.

"Why did you have to do that? Now I will have to copy the whole paper."

"Go ahead – goody two shoes," Michael said as he resumed his ball tossing and walked off. Ellen dried her tears, pulled out a clean sheet of paper and rewrote her homework.

Once finished, she wandered out into the backyard and noticed Grandma Lil sitting in her usual chair near the door. "Hi Grandma, she called out dutifully announcing her presence so as not to embarrass or startle her blind grandmother as she had been taught.

"Hi Ellen, do you want to come sit with me?" Grandma Lil motioned to her lap.

"Sure Grandma." Ellen hopped on Lil's lap and her grandmother gave her a hug.

"How was school today?"

"It was okay."

"Did you learn anything new?"

"We did some math. I like math. We are working on subtraction."

"Good for you."

"Grandma, why do boys have to be so mean?"

"What boys, Ellen?"

"Well…, Ellen began biting her thumbnail, …. Michael. He just tore my math homework for no reason. I had to start it all over again."

"Michael just likes to pick on you Ellen."

"Why?"

"I don't know dear. He just does." Grandma paused thinking that Michael should be more careful with his sister. "You know, Ellen, you have a very big nose!" Grandma said playfully feeling around Ellen's nose and measuring it with her fingers.

"I do not. There is nothing wrong with my nose Grandma," Ellen said mock indignantly. "Compare it with yours. You will see that it is nice and small," Ellen said giggling.

"Oh. I see what you mean Ellen. It feels just right," she said measuring with her forefinger from bridge to tip

Later that evening as Ellen pulled on her pajama bottoms, Michael barged into her bedroom grinning as he caught her standing by the closet door.

"I would be careful if I were you," he warned motioning to the open closet.

"What do you want Michael?"

"The ghosts up there," he said pointing up the stairs within her closet that led up to the attic, "do not like little girls."

"Michael, stop it!" Ellen cried. "No ghosts are up there. Daddy showed me. It is just filled with books and things."

"Ellen, the ghosts are up there and they will come out and get you," he snickered.

"Stop it Michael!" Ellen yelled. "Stop scaring me!"

Chuckling, Michael walked out of the room.

"What is going on in there Ellen?" Sandra called from down the hallway. A few moments later she appeared at Ellen's door. Her angry gaze zoomed in on Ellen standing by the closet. "What are you screaming about?"

"Mommy, Michael was in here and he was scaring me about ghosts in the attic again," she sniffed.

"That's enough Ellen. There are no ghosts. You have to stop screaming all the time. Just ignore Michael when he bothers you."

Ellen plopped down on the bed and started to cry in earnest. Sandra had left the room.

That night, Jay arrived home from work and he made his way up to Ellen's room just in time to wish her a goodnight and tuck her in.

"How's my girl?" He asked as he entered.

"Hi Daddy," she said with a huge smile, "did you have a good day?"

"Yes, I did. How was school?"

"It was good. I like math. We learned some more subtraction today."

"That's my girl."

"Daddy, Michael was bothering me again. He says there are ghosts in the attic," she whispered.

Leaning down to kiss her forehead, he quietly said, "You know there are no ghosts. Do you want me to take you upstairs and show you again?"

"Yes," she said beginning to tremble. My big, strong Daddy will protect me, she thought as she reached out.

"Here we go," Jay said as he scooped Ellen up in a big bear hug and carried her over to her closet. He put her down and took her hand in his as he opened the door and turned on the light switch just inside the door. Both the stairs and attic lit up. "Let's go see all the silly junk in the attic," he said cheerfully.

Jay led Ellen up the short, narrow flight of stairs. As they reached the top, Jay picked her up again. "See Ellen, look around," he said pointing. "Nothing is here except for old books and clothes and discarded things," he said as he carried her around the small attic area. He bent down as they went so they could peek around the objects scattered around. Jay had to crouch down as they rounded the corners of the room, because the ceiling was slanted.

"No ghosts anywhere," he stated as he hugged Ellen close and gave her a soft kiss on the cheek. "What do you see, Ellen?"

"I don't see any ghosts," she murmured, "but Michael said they don't like little girls and that they will come and get me."

"Michael is just trying to scare you. He's making things up. We have looked all over and there are no ghosts. Your Daddy would not lie to you. You are seeing it for yourself. Let's look again." He took her all around the room one last time and then they made their way downstairs.

As Jay tucked Ellen in her bed, he made sure she had her favorite stuffed bunny. He leaned over and kissed her cheeks and then her nose. "You are safe here," he reassured her. "Sleep well, my little girl. I love you."

"I love you too Daddy," she said as she reached up for another hug.

As Jay turned off the light, he frowned as he noticed Ellen had pulled her bunny close and put her thumb in her mouth. I need to have a talk with Michael, he thought.

Chapter Nineteen

October 1973

Mrs. Autumn, Ellen's fifth grade teacher, reviewed the poetry assignments the children turned in that day. Ellen was a good student who was particularly enthusiastic about the poetry unit. Picking up Ellen's paper, Mrs. Autumn read:

I have a second mother out there,
but don't know who she is.
She could be young and beautiful,
Or even in show biz.

I wonder if she thinks of me,
Sometimes when by herself.
Does she ponder,
If I've grown in health.

I really sit and muse
What kind of woman she.
To give me up for adoption,
Who could she possibly be?

I don't know if I will meet her,
Many years from today.
Our paths may meet on the street,
Oh what would we say?

Touched, Mrs. Autumn marked the paper with an A. She and her husband had a social connection through mutual friends with Ellen's parents, and she was aware that Ellen was adopted. Briefly, she considered mentioning the poem to Sandra and Jay, but then decided that Ellen would do so if she wished.

At the same time, across town at Ellen's house, she and Debbie animatedly discussed an after school movie as they watched. Adoption seemed to be the theme of the day, because the movie depicted the struggle of a teenage girl adoptee that searched for and found her birth mother.

"Don't you think it's cool that she found the letter with her real mother's name in that book?" Debbie asked Ellen during the commercial interruption.

"Yeah, but I don't understand why her adopted mother didn't know about it. Who else would have put it in her drawer?"

"That is weird. Maybe the adopted mother forgot about it."

"I think something that important would be hard to forget about."

The commercial was over and the girls continued watching.

"She's really brave to go all by herself to see her birth mother!" Ellen exclaimed after the next segment of the movie revealed the girl's plan to travel by bus alone and confront her biological mother. "Do you think her birth mother will be happy to see her?"

"Yeah I do. I think she will be really excited and happy," Debbie said confidently.

The girls continued watching and were stunned when the movie took an unexpected turn.

"That's horrible! I just can't believe it! It's so sad!" Debbie cried out.

"That is the saddest thing ever," Ellen said emotionally shaken. "I know it's just a movie, but I never thought that a birth mother would slam the door in her daughter's face like that." Ellen did not think she would ever forget the movie mother's words, "I have a family and you are not part of it!" Ellen envisioned herself in the same situation and decided then and there that she would never try to find her birth mother. It would be too terrible to have her mother slam the door in her face and utter those words. She would never risk getting as hurt as the girl in the story. She would never take such a chance.

Later after Debbie left, Ellen looked up from the homework assignment she was completing when Michael walked by her room. "Michael, can I ask you a question?" Ellen called as she walked to the hallway.

"What's up?"

"I was wondering how Mommy and Daddy decided to adopt me. How did they choose me?" Ellen asked hopefully.

"Well squirt, it was simple. There was a whole room of babies…."

Hanging on every word, she interjected, "Was I the cutest one or the sweetest?"

"Not exactly….they wanted a girl, you see, and…" He paused for effect. "And you were… the only girl."

Deflated Ellen watched Michael walk down the hallway to his room.

Ellen lay in bed that night deeply disturbed by the movie she had seen earlier. She did not want to hurt her Mommy and Daddy by asking about her birth family, but she was very curious. It seemed that things came up all the time. She remembered the other day when the lady at the department store told her she looked just like her mommy. Mommy just smiled and thanked the lady, but Ellen knew it was impossible and she wondered if there really was someone out in the world that she did look just like. Ellen did have similar coloring to her mother, but she was very aware that this was accidental. She noticed how her friends and their parents and even their siblings resembled one another, and it always hit a sad chord within her. Every day it brought home to her that Michael was a birth child and she was not. He fit right in to Daddy's side of the family with their large body frames, big hands and size thirteen feet. She was petite and small, unlike anyone else. Ellen fell asleep wishing she could talk to her parents about all this, but knew that she could not.

***

Later that same year, Ellen was nearing the end of fifth grade and elementary school. She was having trouble at school with one of the children; picked on for her outdated clothing. She was the very youngest of the children of her parents and their close friends by at least five years. She believed that her parents had kept trying for another birth child before finally deciding to adopt her. Although she figured that it took a long time, in actuality she knew nothing definitively, since the topic was not ever addressed in her presence. Regardless, the big age difference did set Ellen apart but gave her parents the advantage of lots of old hand me down clothes from her friends' children, a big cost savings for them. Truly Ellen's attire was years outdated, but her parents did not realize that a ten-year old would care or that the other children might ostracize her for it. Unfortunately, that is what came to pass. Little ten-year old Ellen, petite and very shy, was challenged to a fight by the bully of the class. Miserably, she made her way home from school to try and figure out what she was going to do. She turned to Michael, her big brother who by then was a senior in high school, for help.

"Michael, can I come in?" Ellen asked as she knocked on Michael's door. "It's important!"

"Okay. Come in," he called back.

"Michael, I have a big problem," Ellen started. "I don't know what to do."

"What's the matter?" he asked impatiently but then he became somewhat concerned as he looked up and saw Ellen's panicked expression. He crossed the room and turned down the stereo. "American Pie" was playing.

"There is this girl at school, Pat Shipton, who is picking on me. She says my clothes are terrible and that I look disgusting. I know the clothes are yucky, and I have told Mommy and Daddy, but they say that the clothes are fine and serviceable."

"Yeah. So."

"Well.... She keeps pushing me and taunting me, but today was the worst. She challenged me to a fight tomorrow!" Hitting her limit, Ellen started to cry.

"Whoa, Ellen." He said getting up. "A fight. Hold on. It will be okay," he said thinking. "I'll teach you how to fight."

"You will. Really?" Ellen said looking up with hope.

"Yes. I'll show you some moves. You need to stand up for yourself. Like this." For the next half an hour Michael taught Ellen how to hold her hands up, then move her feet around.

"Ellen, remember, you might get hit and it will hurt. But if you stand up to her by showing up and trying to fight, that will be very brave."

"Thank you, thank you Michael," she said as she hugged him and surprisingly he let her.

Just like in the movies, the next day came and Ellen showed up at the appointed location on the path by the playground. She had her friends Debbie, Linda and Julie with her. Pat appeared also with her compatriots, surprised to see that Ellen had not backed down. Terrified, Ellen focused on remembering Michael's instructions. She moved into her fighting stance and put her fists up. She did not realize that she actually looked a bit scary. Pat backed up a pace when it sunk in that Ellen was prepared and ready to fight. She had figured Ellen either would not show up at all or back down.

"You are such a baby. I don't want to fight babies." Pat announced to the crowd. Then, she turned and walked away.

Debbie, Linda and Julie ran and surrounded the startled but amazingly relieved Ellen. They were all talking and laughing at once. "Michael sure knew what to do!" exclaimed Ellen. "I can't wait to go home and tell him what happened!"

***

Maybe she's a prostitute!" Julie exclaimed. "I heard that prostitutes get pregnant a lot."

"I don't know," shuddered Ellen. "I hope not." The girls had advanced to the seventh grade and they had learned a new word. Ellen was not too enthused about this idea. She knew that her friends were not trying to upset her, but the concept was disturbing.

"Well, she wouldn't know which guy was the father and she wouldn't be able to support you, so she would have to put you up for adoption," Julie reasoned out with her seventh grade logic as Linda and Debbie shook their heads in agreement.

"I still think she was just a young girl who got pregnant by mistake," Ellen said quietly. She figured that her biological mother must have gotten pregnant by accident, because that explained why she had chosen to give her up. Over time, Ellen had gathered enough information from various relatives to determine that she wasn't a particularly difficult baby. If she wasn't a bad baby, there must have been another reason that her parents had put her up for adoption.

"That could be too," Julie admitted.

The girls switched to the topic of Peter Frampton and Ellen chimed in with relief. She would much rather talk about music.

133

Chapter Twenty

June 1978

"Daddy, how does it feel to have your baby in high school?" Ellen asked as she walked up behind Jay who was relaxing on a folding chair in the back yard. She noticed that the summer grass was getting rather high – almost time for cutting again, and the big oak tree she climbed every summer, her favorite hiding place until Michael went off to college, was in bloom. Ellen placed her hands on her father's shoulders and rubbed.

"Hmmm," he said enjoying the massage. "I don't know. How did the years fly by?"

"I don't think they've gone quickly. This school year was endless!" Ellen exclaimed hugging her father from behind. As she did so, she noticed a peculiar thing, a lone gray strand in her father's thick brown wavy hair. I guess he's getting older too, Ellen thought. Brushing the stray and unwelcome thought aside she said, "I'm off to the end of the year party at Julie's. I have a ride home tonight, but remember I have Sherri's sweet sixteen tomorrow morning. Don't forget I need to be there by 11:30."

"I won't. I'll be here by 11:00 to take you."

"Thanks, Daddy. I love you so much," she said giving him a kiss on the cheek and walking toward the alley.

"Love you too, little girl. Have fun."

"Uncle Hershel, do you have time to take me to the party?" Ellen said anxiously, the phone pressed firmly against her ear. Fifteen year old Ellen was very excited to attend her first sweet sixteen party. "The party has already started," she said sadly. "I don't know where Daddy is. He said he would be here by 11:00."

"Don't worry, I'll be right over. Where's the party?"

"Off of Freedom Road at the Canista Restaurant."

No sooner had Ellen arrived at the party and Uncle Hershel had left, Sherri's mother tapped Ellen on the shoulder, "I received a call from a friend of your mother, Mrs. Hillman, and she said to tell you to get ready to leave. Lisa, her daughter, will be picking you up."

"I don't understand. I just got here."

"Ellen, dear," she said something has happened to your father and Lisa is to take you to the hospital."

"Daddy?"

Lisa arrived at just that moment. Rushing up behind Ellen and Sherri's mother she said, "Yes, your father. I need to take you right away. Come with me Ellen."

In a blur, Lisa guided Ellen to the car. The hospital, a drive of just a few minutes, was in view before Ellen could begin to fathom what was happening. Lisa pulled the car up to the hospital entrance, quickly ran around to Ellen's side of the car and guided Ellen to the front door just as Dr. Greene, Barbara's husband and the family physician, rushed outside. "Thank you Lisa. I'll take her from here," he said.

As the two made their way inside, Dr. Greene dressed in his hospital whites with an especially morose expression briefly stopped, turned toward Ellen and bluntly stated, "Ellen, your father had a heart attack and he died."

"What? Why would you say such a thing?" Ellen responded, shocked by the abrupt announcement. Taking in the white expansive walls of the long corridor, the firm and almost painful grasp of Dr. Greene, the antiseptic smell surrounding her, her brain tried to catch up. As they reached the end of the corridor, she recognized her mother and brother coming toward her, arms outstretched, tears flowing. What is wrong with everyone? She thought as she turned and ran back the way she had come. But as she hesitated once outside, they caught her and grabbed onto her and cried on her. Ellen couldn't make sense of their words, although she knew – she knew that her world had just been turned upside down and nothing would ever be the same.

The ride home was torturous as Diana, Michael's fiancée, tried to drive them home without incident, Michael and Sandra wailed, and Ellen stared out the window immobile.

Detached, Ellen watched as her mother, Sandra, approached Grandma Lil resting in her chair by the backdoor outside their house on Mill Street. "Mother," Sandra sobbed reaching out to her, "Jay died this morning. He had a heart attack."

"Oh my Lord – NO!" Grandma Lil screamed. "My Jay, my Jay, my Jay – NOOOOOO!" Sandra pulled her mother inside the house, while Ellen viewed the exchange in horror.

Passing the inconsolable pair on her way through the kitchen, Ellen ran up to her room and quietly closed the door. She sat on the red carpet and flicked the annoyingly bright strands back and forth with her hand. She didn't know what to do. She sat and she sat and then finally she picked up the phone by her bed.

She called her friend, Julie. "Julie," she whispered unsure of herself, "my father died this morning." Hearing her own words from her own lips finally broke the defensive shield of disbelief her mind had created, the tears began to flow, and she cried from the depths of a fifteen year old girl's heart for the father she loved dearly. She cried and cried. She cried for the past and she cried for the future. Daddy was her rock, he was the one who took interest in her little world. What would life be like now without him? Her head pounded with the implausible thoughts.

Following Jewish custom, Jay's funeral was the very next day, the significance of the loss brutally compounded by the fact that it was Father's Day. It should have been a day of another botched cookout due to rain, the Brenner family's constant joke. It should have been a day to celebrate and remember Ellen's amazing, warm, loving, incredible father - her handmade card saying such in swirling girly lettering lay waiting on her desk for a father that would never read it. Instead there she stood at the graveside ceremony beneath a threatening sky, as sun and clouds warred with each other over that tiny spot in the cosmos, and many of their family and friends participated in the final tribute to a man whose time was short on this earth but who left this world well-loved and truly missed.

"Ellen, come stand here by me," Uncle Hershel said seeing her confusion and noticing that Sandra, surrounded by her close friends, was too distraught to look out for Ellen, and Michael, crying unabashedly, held tight to his fiancée Diana. This was Ellen's very first experience at a funeral. Gratefully, she grabbed onto Uncle Hershel's hand.

"Do you hear the wonderful things being said about your father?"

"Yeah."

"By listening, you may feel a tiny bit better. Look at all the people who cared and loved him."

"I see," she replied in a small voice.

Unprepared, but who ever is, and jarred to the core by the clumping sound and gruesome image of earth building and covering the simple coffin, Ellen wrapped her arms around Uncle Hershel and huddled close. "It will be over soon," he soothed.

Momentarily leaving her sister, Ellen's Grandma Lil, seated but somewhat composed, Aunt Shirley moved to Ellen's other side and wrapped her arm around her as well. "Oh dear Ellen, your father loved you so much," Aunt Shirley sobbed as she whispered in her ear.

In accordance with conservative Jewish custom, a three day shiva (memorial) was observed on Mill Street. Family, friends, and acquaintances flowed through the house offering condolences and cherished memories, distracting the mourners and keeping them busy. Time moved just a bit, providing the mourners a slice of distance from the tragedy and newness of loss.

Ellen was very busy with the young people, who on their own or pressed by parents to do the right thing, made their shiva calls. As she moved through the living room on the second day, she heard two visitors speaking.

"You know, don't you, that Ellen was adopted. Sandra and Jay had trouble after Michael was born."

"Oh. I never knew. Now that you mention it, she doesn't look much like anyone in either family. I used to think she looked like Sandra, but not anymore."

Saddened by the gossiping pair, Ellen made her way through the crowd to the first floor bathroom. She plopped down on the closed toilet seat. I was still Daddy's girl, she thought. He always loved me the same as if I had been his biological daughter, she told herself. But Daddy was gone and their words hurt – made her feel lost and alone and placed outside her own family. Hugging herself, she cried quietly as she rocked back and forth on the seat.

Chapter Twenty-One

June 1979

"Life in my house is dark that's the only way to describe it," sixteen year old Ellen began. Almost a year to the day since her father had died, Ellen confided in her friend Sherri, her one friend from a different high school and whose sweet sixteen party she had almost attended a whole year ago. "I'm really sorry I haven't been a better friend this past year," Ellen continued as she leaned against the trunk of her favorite oak tree in the backyard, the same tree she had climbed to read and escape from household drama until the age of thirteen. "Michael escaped," Ellen said, brushing her overgrown bangs out of her eyes with a flick of her fingers. "He graduated college right before Daddy died. He moved out and got a job with an insurance company, and he and Diana got engaged – they just got married a few weeks ago. They live in Randallstown. So he wasn't here to see how bad things were at home. It was tough with Grandma and Mom and me trying to cope. Grandma Lil's hearing keeps getting worse. Along with her blindness, the deafness is making it really hard for her. She stays in her room most of the time."

"What about your mother?" Sherri asked stretching her jean-clad legs out toward the tree as she sat facing Ellen.

"Mom is basically absent. Her friends take amazing care of her and whisk her away constantly trying to cheer her up and look after her. And I babysit Grandma a lot. She needs looking after more and more. Sherri, I really don't mind staying with Grandma, because it's so hard for me to connect with kids my age. I just can't get worked up about the latest movie or boys or you know."

"I think I get it – kind of, but I was around Ellen. You could have talked to me."

"I know," Ellen said embarrassed yet trying to make her friend understand. "Thanks. I guess I wasn't ready to share much. We talked on the phone a few times, remember? Anyway, I'm glad tenth grade is over. It was a nightmare! I botched my classes, had trouble with the teachers, and attempted to run for school office – with no clue how to do it without making a fool of myself. In fact, I have no idea why I wanted to run at all." Ellen raked her hand through her short layered hair trying to get to her point. "It's hard to explain… I think that I aged. I really feel older than all my friends and classmates – please don't take offense," she said looking at her friend. "All year I felt that I had responsibilities at home and didn't have time for petty high school drama. It was dark and dismal here, and I missed Daddy more than anything."

"Your father was very nice, Ellen."

"Yeah, he was a really good man and a great father. His death makes me incredibly hurt and angry. I'm angry with everything and especially with God. How could He take such a good person away and make him leave us? Daddy was only 51 and I was only 15, Sherri. It makes no sense!"

And it didn't, but life moved on as is the case. That very week, Sandra was stopped in the milk aisle at the supermarket by a family acquaintance, Laura Sachs.

"Sandra, hello," Laura called as she approached Sandra. "How are you and how is your daughter, Ellen? Such a nice girl! She and my Noah are very good friends, as you must know," Laura gushed.

"Ellen is fine, thank you. She's working at the bagel store, keeping herself busy." Sandra replied hurriedly. "Sorry to rush off, but I must get home. Mother will be waiting for dinner and I needed to pick up a few things."

"I understand. Good to see you Sandra. Please say hi to Ellen for us," Laura said with a wave.

That evening, Laura found her eldest son Noah at the kitchen table eating a pile of sandwiches and a mound of potato chips as she arrived home from the supermarket.

"Please help me with the bags, Noah," Laura said placing the two filled paper bags she had carried in onto the counter.

Without a word, Noah left his meal and brought in the bags. Returning to his seat and resuming his dinner, Laura took stock of her eldest son as she put away the groceries. Dressed in a Colts decorated tee-shirt and white shorts dirty from his busy day as a summer tennis instructor at the local high school, Noah downed a tall glass of soda. Always the athlete, Laura noticed that as usual a basketball lay on the floor beside his seat. He was average height 5'9", skinny build but toned and tanned from innumerable hours on the basketball and tennis courts. He had medium brown extremely curly hair to the point of frizzy which she noted looked very nice after the recent trim. Smiling she said, "Noah, guess who I ran into today?"

"I don't know, Mom. Who?"

Twenty questions?"

With stunning bright blue eyes, Noah looked up from his dinner and replied, "Mom, I really can't manage twenty questions right now. How about you just tell me?"

"Okay. Okay. I ran into Sandra Brenner, Ellen's mother."

"That's nice. How is Ellen?" Noah said with true interest. "I haven't spoken to her in awhile. I wonder how she's doing." He paused wrinkling his brow, then continued, "I think the last time I saw her was at her father's funeral."

"Sandra said she is doing okay. She's working at the bagel store."

"That's good. Maybe I'll stop in and see her."

Noah really did want to know how Ellen was doing, so that very night after a quick shower and change, he drove his green three-on-the-tree Chevy Nova over to the bagel store, which took a quick five minutes, hoping to find Ellen working the evening shift.

"Oh, hi Noah. How are you? It's so nice to see you," Ellen said cheerfully as Noah took a stool by the counter.

"Hi Ellen. I'm good. Your mother told my mother you were working here when they ran into each other at the supermarket. I thought I would come by and see how you're doing?"

"I'm fine. The work here is pretty good. It's hard to believe they let me prepare food, the one who can't cook anything. Luckily, the boss only yells at me every other day," Ellen said laughing at herself and smiling at Noah. Ellen was truly happy to see her friend Noah. They had been summer buddies for years, although when she thought about the summer before, the summer when her father died, she realized that she hadn't really spent time with Noah in quite a while. "It really is nice to see you Noah. It's been a long time. Hey, how was your first year of college?"

"I liked it. I already changed my major cause had a little glitch with a Bio class, but since then everything is great."

Fortunately, business was slow at the store, so the two talked and caught up with each other's lives while Ellen cleaned and straightened up. Before long Noah came to a decision, "Ellen would you like to go watch the fireworks at the harbor on the fourth of July with me?" he asked.

"Sure. That's sounds like fun," Ellen responded happily. "I think I'm scheduled to work that night, but I'll see if I can find someone to switch with me."

"Great. I'll call you in a few days."

Ellen worked out her schedule at the bagel store and confirmed the date with Noah. The fourth came and as she watched Noah walk up the path to her house, she was surprised. Is that a kippah (ritual headcovering) on his head? Quickly thinking back, Ellen realized that Noah had always worn a baseball cap; his head had always been covered. Suddenly, she understood that the hat wasn't just for the sun but had religious significance. How did I never know that Noah was religious? She thought. Ellen had been raised knowledgeable of the Jewish holidays but secular in practice. She often had Friday night dinners at her Aunt Shirley and Uncle Hershel's home where they kept somewhat kosher – although the crabs in the basement once a year was a spectacularly curious thing – and she had been Bat Mitzvahed and gone to Hebrew school even extra years to be Confirmed, but she knew few boys who wore a kippah outside of the synagogue. She found it extremely interesting that she didn't know, yet she was not fazed by the revelation either. Noah was Noah, and that meant she would have a good time with her friend.

"Hi Ellen. Are you up for a movie instead? I think the fireworks are rained out," Noah said as Ellen ushered him into the living room.

"Sure. What movie do you have in mind?" Ellen replied.

"I thought maybe we could go see *The In-Laws*. With Alan Arkin and Peter Falk starring as the soon to be in-laws, it's supposed to be very funny."

"Great. I like comedies."

No fireworks that night, but the movie proved to be a harbinger of things to come. For the next five years, while Noah finished college and then pharmacy graduate school and Ellen worked her way through high school and then college, Ellen and Noah dated steadily right up until their marriage in 1984 when Sandra Brenner became in-laws with Laura Sachs.

"Mrs. Brenner," Noah asked Ellen's mother a few weeks before the wedding, "since Ellen is adopted, how do you know that she is Jewish? I'm only asking because I spoke to Rabbi Feinberg who will be marrying us, and he needs some sort of proof. I don't want to upset you in any way."

"Well... ," Sandra replied. "All I know is that the Jewish Adoption Center told me she was Jewish. I believe they only adopt Jewish babies. I hope that will be sufficient for the rabbi."

"Thank you. I will pass the information on."

"Did you speak to Ellen about this?"

"No, I didn't. I came to you first."

"Good. She wouldn't have any idea. It is best that you came to me."

Chapter Twenty-Two

May 1986

Ellen was a young, married woman of 22 in the spring of 1986, she was changing and growing, both literally because she was into the second trimester of her pregnancy with their first child and also spiritually. She began to attend her first formal Judaism classes since her Hebrew school days. The classes, held in a local Orthodox synagogue, were part of an outreach initiative in the community and were much different for Ellen, because they dealt with the laws and practices of Judaism from an Orthodox perspective. The Hebrew school classes had been geared toward a younger audience, much more elementary in nature and from a Conservative slant.

Ellen enjoyed the classes and felt an increased connection with Judaism. Even more importantly, she gained confidence in her understanding of the religion and the specifics of observance and began to close the gap between the education she had received and the amount of knowledge she needed for her new, more traditional, way of life. She loved coming home and discussing the new concepts with Noah.

One particularly bright and sunny day as she sat in the small classroom in a standard issue folding chair listening attentively to a lecture on an array of brief subjects, her attention was riveted as the topic of adoption was brought up.

"It is inadvisable to adopt a Jewish baby, because the baby may have been conceived by an adulterous union," the teacher, a learned middle-aged man with a trimmed beard and large black kippah said in a matter of fact manner. "This causes the baby to be a special status of mamzer (loosely translated as bastard), and the baby along with its progeny would be mamzerim (plural) until the tenth generation."

In stunned silence Ellen grappled with the statement. The teacher continued to ramble on, but she was shaken to the core. What did she know about her birth? Virtually nothing. Married, pregnant and frantic that her baby would be labeled a mamzer by all, Ellen began to tremble. What would this do to my children? What did this actually mean in the 20th century? She became distraught as the thoughts swirled in her head. Did Noah know of such things? How could he have taken such a risk? What should they do? How could this teacher make such an incredibly harsh statement as if no one would possibly be affected? Was this for real? Fortunately the class broke for a recess, and she ran out of the building – never to return to those classes.

Ellen was frantic. She didn't know what to do. No Judaic concept she had learned included convicting a child for its parents' sins for multiple generations. This was a faith challenge to be sure, and she drove white-knuckled the mile distance home attempting extreme caution while tears blurred her vision. Ellen called Noah. In broken sobs and quite incoherently, she began, "I was just in class Noah, and the teacher said that our baby may be a mamzer and then our children and grandchildren until the tenth generation will be mamzerim. Could this be true?"

"Ellen, I can hardly understand you. Please calm down. It isn't good for you to get so upset. What are you saying about our children?"

Taking a deep breath, Ellen began again, "I was just in class and the teacher said Jewish people should not adopt Jewish babies!"

"What did he say was the reason?" Noah asked confused.

"He said that the baby could be a mamzer if the mother had an illicit relationship. What does that mean really?"

"Hold on just a minute - sorry - I have a line of customers." Shortly he returned. "Sorry, it's so busy!" Taking a deep breath he said, "There are certain relationships that are forbidden in Jewish law. One example is a married woman with a man not her husband." He paused and held the phone away from his ear. Ellen heard the pharmacy technician speaking to him. Returning to the conversation, Noah said hurriedly, "Ellen, I can't explain everything right now. There is so much more to this. I need you to lie down and rest. I'll be home in just a few hours, and I'll try to explain everything. Please don't worry. All will be fine."

"Do you truly think so?"

"Yes, of course. We will see our way through this. Now please go rest for yourself and the baby. Tell me you will."

"Ok. I'll rest and see you soon. Please come right home."

Rushing in the door, Noah looked around the house for Ellen. He was relieved to find her resting on the sofa in the den with the stereo softly playing. He recognized the song "Against All Odds" and remembered seeing the movie by the same title with Ellen. "Ellen, I'm home," Noah whispered as he knelt beside her.

"Good. I am so glad to see you," she said reaching for a hug. Holding back the tears that threatened to begin anew, she prompted, "Tell me more about this crazy idea. Wouldn't it make more sense for Jewish people to adopt Jewish babies, so the babies would remain Jewish? I can't wrap my head around this thing," Ellen sniffed.

"Sweetheart, you have a good point for sure and I think most people would agree," Noah said taking a seat on the sofa. He sidled close to Ellen and softly stroked her hand as he continued to explain, "Sometimes halacha (Jewish law) is complicated. The teacher did a very misguided thing today by not explaining fully."

"He sure did. What if there were other people in the class like me? I don't know what else he may have said that hurt others as much as this affected me," Ellen said miserably.

"Again, you have a valid point, but we can't do much about him now. I think everything is fine with us and our baby. To be a mamzer, a child has to be a result of an illicit union, one not allowed by Jewish law, for example a sister and brother or a married woman with a man other than her husband."

"I don't know if my mother was married or not," Ellen said shaking her head in frustration as she wondered for the millionth time why her parents failed to tell her anything substantial about her adoption.

"That's true, but even if your mother was married and she was living with her husband, the Jewish ruling would probably be that you were the product of the marriage. Even if the married couple were estranged or divorced, as long as the husband and wife had an opportunity to be together within a twelve month time period, the baby would be attributed to the husband.

"Twelve months?"

"Yes. I believe that our rabbis of old believed there had been cases of fetuses being in the womb for up to twelve months."

"I guess that helps more people to avoid this negative identification."

"Yes, and therefore the probability that we have a problem is very low. I really believe everything will be fine. I have faith."

"I know you do and that helps me," she said squeezing his hand for emphasis.

"Also, Ellen, mamzerim are full class Jewish citizens, meaning they have the same rights and opportunities. They can lead services in synagogue, inherit property and hold positions of authority. Because their children will continue to be termed mamzer, the only thing they are prohibited from doing is marrying regular status Jewish mates."

"What? That's terrible. How will they find anyone to marry?"

"I have heard that there is a network of people and quietly couples get together. In addition, they are allowed to marry Jewish converts."

"Is there any way for someone to break the chain and become a regular Jew?"

"I think I once learned that the male mamzer cannot change his own status, but his male child can attain regular status if he marries a non-Jewish woman. The children would not be Jewish at birth, because religious identity follows the mother. The children would then be converted to Judaism and at that point they would not be mamzerim, they would have regular Jewish status."

"It sounds like the religion is forcing these people to intermarry."

"It is complicated, but the point is to deter people from committing adultery in the first place, to force them to think about their future generations and act appropriately."

"Noah, it's still so hard to understand, and it doesn't actually help our children. What are we supposed to do? What are adopted people supposed to do?" Ellen said jumping up. Pacing, she began to rail, "All I know is that adoptions in this country protect the privacy of the biological mother and the adoptive parents. The adopted child has no rights and unless someone feels like giving them information or they manage an expensive and difficult search process, they're left in precarious situations like this. It is completely unconscionable!" Ellen said as she continued to pace back and forth. Noah slumped down in the sofa forcing down his own annoyance as he watched her. It was not the first time he had heard Ellen express her irritation over the inequity of adoptees' rights, and he knew it would not be the last. Impotent to change the situation, he felt her pain and knew her pain to be real. As her advocate and partner, he profoundly wished he could do more to help her.

It was Noah's explanation, along with his deep seated belief that all would work out and the faith to stand by that assertion, that pulled Ellen through the next few days.

The following Sabbath, Ellen and Noah had lunch with Noah's sister, Sara and brother-in-law, Sam. Once the group was seated at the festive meal, Ellen, who was finding it difficult to focus on anything but the mamzer issue, immediately blurted out the story while subconsciously patting her growing belly.

"Why don't you contact the Jewish Adoption Center and see what information they can give you. They have been the most prominent agency in Baltimore for handling Jewish children," Sam suggested.

"That's actually a great idea," Ellen responded. "I know for sure that I was adopted in Baltimore. I must've been adopted through that agency. That's something proactive - yes. I can handle anything life throws my way with a plan. Thanks, Sam. What a great idea!"

First thing the following Monday morning, Ellen called into work and requested a few hours of personal leave, then she drove the family's white minivan the short ten minutes to the Jewish Adoption Center on Park Avenue. Fortunately a caseworker was available to meet with her even though she had no appointment.

"What kind of information are you hoping to find, Mrs. Sachs?" the caseworker, Mrs. Weiss asked.

"I would love to find out the relationship of my parents, were they married or single. Also, I'd like to know if there are any medical considerations or illnesses that run in the family," Ellen replied. "Is that the kind of information you may have in the file?"

"Yes. We certainly should have information on marital status and medical history. Why do you want this information?" Mrs. Weiss inquired. "This is a standard question that we ask everyone."

"The doctors at my OB office keep asking me for medical history. Every month they annoy and worry me by asking the same question. Every month, I tell them that I don't know my medical history, because I am adopted – they leave the area blank in their files and then wonder why it's blank – so they repeatedly ask me. I would love to answer their question once and for all." Ellen had thought out her response ahead of time. She left out the true impetus for her visit, because she did not feel up to explaining the whole mamzer thing – it sounded and was extreme by her account.

"Are you hoping to find or contact your biological mother or parents?"

"No. Honestly, I have no desire to find them. I'm not ready to open myself up for that at this time."

"Well Mrs. Sachs, I am sure that we can help you. What you seek is called non-identifying information. I will look up your file and write a report of any information that can be shared without including anything that identifies or would help you to identify your biological parents."

"How soon can you have the report ready?"

"Less than two weeks."

"Perfect. Thank you, Mrs. Weiss," Ellen said, mentally preparing herself for the wait.

***

Ellen stayed as calm as possible aided by Noah's constant reassurances, and the two weeks did pass. She returned to the Jewish Adoption Center, and Mrs. Weiss handed her a two page typewritten report in paragraph form that included information about Ellen's biological mother, brief information on her background which included the crucial statement that she was unmarried at the time of Ellen's birth – big news that put the mamzer issue to rest. Fortunately, single women were not included in the list of illicit relationships regardless of the man's marital status. In addition, the report stated that Ellen's mother had been Bat Mitzvahed, and sadly that both her parents had died when she was young, her mother when she was seven and her father when she was 18. The only health details were that some high and low blood pressure ran in the family. No information was given at all on her father. Since the father's information was unnecessary for the mamzer issue, Ellen barely noticed the absence. Ellen was extremely satisfied with the report, because it sufficiently addressed her two most pressing concerns, the reasons that she had approached the Jewish Adoption Center. Carefully, she placed the report in the family safe deposit box at the bank for safekeeping. You never know when it might be needed, she thought.

Following the resolution of the traumatic mamzer issue, which thankfully did not impact Ellen's health, her pregnancy proceeded without note. Noah and Ellen were blessed with three daughters in quick succession. With each birth, Ellen was deeply moved and comforted by the realization that she finally had family with blood ties, people she loved and were known to her that shared her DNA. She could see her resemblance in others for the first time. The Sachs family was blessed with more ups than downs, years filled with happy children and adoring parents.

Chapter Twenty-Three

November 1996

The years had been joyfully filled with children and child-rearing. Then, illness took center stage once again. Sandra was diagnosed with pancreatic cancer. Found to be inoperable, chemotherapy was tried, but the cancer proved too advanced. Even though the doctors claimed they had found it early, thanks to Dr. Greene, the progress was rapid and fatal. The night before Sandra's funeral, Ellen couldn't sleep.

"Ellen, what's the matter?" Noah asked as he got into bed hours after Ellen had retired for the evening.

"I've been lying here thinking about Mom. It really is amazing how quickly one dies of pancreatic cancer. The doctors tell you they caught it quickly, but I don't know. Nine months is really fast."

"She did have three nice months in the summer when my mother was in the hospital."

"I know. That was a blessing, and thank God your mother got better. Luckily I finished your mother's birthday present last night. Maybe you should run it over before the funeral."

"It can wait," Noah said. He revised his thought when he looked at Ellen's determined face. "Whatever you want."

"I want her to have the framed collage of her children and grandchildren. Besides, not everyone gets to reach a 70th birthday," Ellen said with emphasis.

"Your mother for example, she would have been 70 next year."

"That's true." After a palpable pause, Ellen said, "Noah, I think I have something to say at the funeral."

"You definitely should speak if you want to. I'll notify the funeral director for you. What do you want to say?"

"Even though my mother and I had a complicated relationship that was often strained and painful for me, I want to thank her for adopting me. It was an amazing thing to do, and I feel my life was completely different than it would have been. Speaking about the adoption is the only thing that is uniquely mine to say. If I don't, then it won't be said."

"That sounds like a good idea. Do you need help writing your speech?"

"No. I think I have it figured out already. I just need to get it down on paper. I think I'll do it now."

The next day, at the funeral chapel, Ellen followed Michael in giving her public remarks. As Ellen noiselessly climbed the four plush carpeted steps up to the platform and walked toward the podium, she pulled her black sweater more tightly around her trying to ward off the pervasive chill that enveloped her. Gazing out at the sea of faces, shivering, but with a strong voice she said, "I want to thank you Mom for adopting me, and along with Daddy bringing me into your home and sharing yourselves and your lives with love and compassion.

It was an extraordinary chesed (kindness) that you did, which I know radically changed the course of my life. It is no small thing to choose to take in a child that is not yours biologically and provide for them in all ways." Nodding toward the covered casket Ellen completed her remarks with heartfelt gratitude, "Thank you, Mom." She looked at the casket that held the remains of the only mother she had known and then out into the huge crowd that caused the funeral home to open both overflow areas of the hall. As she concluded, Ellen felt satisfied that she had achieved her goal by thanking her mother in a way she had never done while her mother had been living. The audibly loud sound of the hushed audience trailed with her as she returned to her seat.

"Your speech was perfect and courageous," Rabbi Berg told Ellen at the shiva house later that day.

"Thank you for that, rabbi. Although, I am certainly not a talented public speaker, I felt it needed to be said. I was the only one who could do it."

"I know you touched many today, Ellen."

***

Shortly after her mother's death, Ellen began a new job in her field of computer programming, a job for the state located at the main office in downtown Baltimore. Two weeks later, she was summoned to her supervisor's office and told to report to the Vital Events office, told to develop a computer application for them that would be explained to her once there, told to use whatever software was left on the computer abandoned by the technical person previously assigned there and told to report the following day. Confused but intrigued, Ellen did as she was told and happily found that the Vital Events office was just seven short minutes' drive from her home and only three minutes to her children's school, a much easier commute and more comfortable office conditions. She also found that Vital Events was the custodian of all birth and death information for the state. Ellen watched as continual lines of applicants requesting birth and death certificates filed past the front counters. She decided to get additional copies of her own children's birth certificates. She did so simply by filling in a request form and paying a fee, no problem. Ellen's birth certificate was not so straightforward, because adoption records were sealed, the original birth certificate replaced by the court approved certificate. She could and did request a birth certificate, but only her adopted name and her adopted parents' names were listed.

"Noah, it's just not fair!" Ellen ranted as she set the table for dinner. Clunking down the dinner plates, she said, "I fill out my paperwork and pay my fee just like everyone else, but everyone else obtains their actual birth certificate and I don't. I get a different version of the truth not the real truth. It isn't fair!"

"I agree, Ellen," Noah said shaking his head sadly as he followed after her with the napkins.

"I don't get it. Kelly, at the office, told me that often the birth date on adoption birth certificates is changed by a day or two. I may not even know my actual birthday. It's pathetic. I feel so resentful. The law seems to protect everyone's rights but mine!"

"Is there a process to open the file – or whatever they do?"

"I think it is just a cross-referenced numbering system. The new record has a number or code linking it to the old number, and I think they only access the old record if there is a court order."

"Ellen, what do you want to find out?"

"I don't know that I want to find out anything," Ellen said collapsing in her chair. "I just feel so cheated by the process and kept in the dark. If my birthday is different than what I have celebrated all my life – I'll be angry. It may sound stupid and probably does, but then I would know absolutely nothing about my birth. All along, I thought I knew at least that tiny bit of information. It's so upsetting!"

"Yes. I see that," Noah said as he moved behind her and massaged her tight neck and shoulders.

***

The seasons came and went and the world entered the new millennium, January 2000. It was a few days before Ellen's birthday. She thought back to that very morning standing by the front door before leaving for work when she had told Noah, "My friends and I used to think about the year 2000 and think how old we would be. Thirty-seven seemed ancient. How is it that it came so fast?"

As she walked up the long hallway toward her office, Ellen met her friend Kelly coming in the opposite direction. With birthday on the brain, Ellen asked, "Kelly, what would I need to do to open my adoption record and get my real birth certificate?"

"By law you need a court order from the court in which you were adopted. Do you know where you were adopted?" Kelly replied, pausing by the copier. She and Ellen occasionally talked about Ellen's adoption and what it truly meant to Ellen. Recently, Kelly had shared stories of her adopted cousin who had repeatedly failed to locate her birth family.

"The adoption agency was in the city, but I lived in the county when I was first brought home."

"I guess it could be either court. Why don't you send a request to both, just a simple statement asking to open the file? I have the names and addresses of the Clerks of the Courts."

"Do you think they will allow me access just for asking?"

"I don't know if they will. Things are changing. I don't think I explained to you when you recently set up the database file, adoptions are now open. Any child born from January 1, 2000 and after can have their birth information from us as soon as they reach 18 years of age. All they will need to do is request it in writing. The law changed and became effective on January 1."

"Does that work for me as well?"

"No. I would have told you if it did, it was not grandfathered in, meaning it does not allow for people born prior to January 1, 2000."

"That's not fair."

"I don't think so either, but the agreement and understanding of the birth mother or birth parents in the past was that the record would be kept confidential. The new law changes that going forward."

"It figures for me, but I'm glad for the young babies of today. Maybe I'll write to the courts. Thanks, Kelly."

"I sent the letters to the courts and I received responses," Ellen said to Noah as he sat reading and relaxing in the den, sprawled in his favorite recliner.

"Well which court was it?"

"Neither, according to them. They both said they didn't have my case in their records."

"That's strange, but could be for the best. Maybe we shouldn't open our lives to possibly harmful influences. You know I don't mean that as badly as it sounds, but I don't want you hurt and maybe it's better while the kids are young to be careful who we let into our lives – especially since you're not so sure you want to know anything."

"I guess so. You are probably right, and you make good points. I think I'll drop the whole thing. My ambivalence always tips the scales," she said shaking her head.

Chapter Twenty-Four

September 2007

The next eleven years rushed past too quickly, and the Sachs girls grew up. Ellen and Noah marveled at the physical similarities and personality traits that each child shared with one or both parents. Rachel, the eldest, was a beautiful, female version of Noah and a definite member of the Sachs clan, although one could easily see glimpses of Ellen in her disposition. Lily, the second born, was Ellen's clone but fortunately shared much of Noah's "go with the flow" type B attitude. When Lily and Ellen's fifth grade school pictures were placed side by side on the dining room table, only the whims of fashion identified daughter from mother. The external mixture of Ellen and Noah came in the lovely form of their youngest daughter, Jill. With a little bit of this side and a little bit of that, Jill was a looker with a uniquely vibrant personality all her own.

By the latter part of 2007, Rachel was finishing college in New York and accepted to a prestigious graduate school for the following year, Lily was working toward her bachelor's degree at university in Israel, and Jill was barreling through high school.

Rachel's boyfriend, Daniel, was also in school in New York finishing up his undergraduate work. They had been dating a few months and were beginning to get serious. It was becoming evident that they both were feeling that they had found their besharet, the perfect one destined for them to marry. In their quest to find out everything they could about one another they spent many hours talking about their lives, their goals, their dreams. One night, as they walked around midtown Manhattan, Rachel mentioned that her mother, Ellen, was adopted to which Daniel, with innocent curiosity, asked her how her mother knew that she was Jewish. It was a simple question, but the answer was really not so simple. Rachel, with total honesty, told Daniel that her mother had always known. With nothing further to add, Rachel directed the conversation to another topic although the adoption one weighed heavily on her mind. Early the next morning before her father went to work, Rachel called him.

"Hello Rachel, how are you?" Noah answered.

"I'm good. Dad, I have a question? I was out with Daniel last night and I mentioned that Mom was adopted. He asked me how we know that she's Jewish. I told him that we've always known, and suddenly I heard how that sounded and even though I think Daniel accepted it, I wasn't so comfortable. Dad, how do we know for sure?"

"Rachel, we know because that's what Mom was told by her adopted family and what was told to her mother and father by the Jewish Adoption Center, the agency that handled the adoption."

"Dad, this is really important. Daniel and I are getting serious. I need to be absolutely sure that I'm Jewish, and I can't know that for a certainty unless we know without question that Mom is Jewish. Would you do some research and make sure that the agency information is enough?"

"Sure. I'll speak to Mom and we'll get back to you."

"Thanks Dad. Do you think Mom will be upset?"

"I don't think so. She'll be okay. Don't worry."

That was on a Friday morning. Noah waited until later that night when he and Ellen were enjoying a particularly quiet Sabbath dinner, just the two of them, before mentioning the conversation with Rachel.

"Ellen, Rachel called early this morning before I left for work."

"That's unusual. Don't you usually speak to her late in the afternoon?"

"Yes, but today she had a specific question."

"Is everything okay? She seemed fine when I spoke to her around lunchtime."

"She is fine, but something has come up." He paused at this point and Ellen's attention was piqued. "She and Daniel were discussing the fact of your adoption and they were wondering how we know for sure that you are Jewish."

"I guess it has always been a fact told to me by my parents," Ellen said succinctly. Noticing Noah's paused reaction, she continued, "Somehow I feel that there is more to this." Ellen had set the table with fine china, crystal glasses and their finest sterling in honor of the Sabbath. Absently mesmerized by the flickering images of the candles of her candelabra as seen through her glass, Ellen wondered where this was going.

"I think there may be," Noah continued, "so I took the liberty of asking Rabbi Golden today what he would need to know in order to marry the kids if and when the time comes."

"To know – do you mean proof of some type. Noah, you know I don't have any real proof. We didn't need any proof when we got married." Unsuccessfully Ellen tried not to become agitated, but she had a terrible sense of foreboding.

"Actually, the issue did come up. I had a discussion with Rabbi Feinberg before he married us. I didn't want to upset you at the time, so I spoke with your mother and she assured me that the Jewish Adoption Center had told her that you were definitely Jewish."

"You did. I never knew. Of course, if you hadn't chosen to tell me, Mom never would. She never talked to me about the adoption."

"I know. I was trying to protect you. Rabbi Feinberg was satisfied with the verbal response from your mother, and the matter was settled quickly. I hope you aren't angry with me. It never came up again until now."

"How incredible that I didn't know a thing nor suspect – of course an Orthodox rabbi would want to make sure we were both Jewish," Ellen reasoned. "I was so young and clueless! With my background, it would never have occurred to me. I did meet with Rabbi Feinberg before we were married as I recall, but I don't remember him asking about my Jewishness."

"I had already spoken to him and we had settled it."

"Ok. Would a statement from him be proof enough?"

"I don't really know for sure. Rabbi Golden is thinking it over. I told him you would call him this week."

"Noah, it's going to be terribly difficult to find proof. Searching for my biological mother would be very hard to do. According to the non-identifying information report from the Jewish Adoption Center, she was an only child with both parents deceased way before the report creation – and that was 20 years ago. She probably has married and has a different last name."

"Let's wait and see what Rabbi Golden finds out."

"I'll call both rabbis' offices this week. Hopefully we won't need to find her at all," Ellen replied with a silent prayer.

Chapter Twenty-Five

First thing Sunday morning, Ellen called Rabbi Feinberg's office. His secretary assured her that they would have no records dating back beyond ten years. Then she spoke briefly with the rabbi, but he had no recollection of any issues to do with her adoption at the time of her marriage. Realizing that this was surely a dead end, she thanked the rabbi and moved on to plan B.

Early Monday morning, Ellen made her way to the Jewish Adoption Center. She was ushered into Mrs. Kaplan, a social worker's, office.

"What can I do for you today, Mrs. Sachs?" Mrs. Kaplan inquired.

"I have a problem and surely hope you can help. I was adopted through your agency and I need proof of my Jewish heritage."

"What kind of proof?"

"I'm not exactly sure. My daughter is soon to be engaged, and my rabbi feels that I need something that definitively states that my mother and her mother before her were Jewish."

"I'm not so sure I can provide you with such a thing. I'm not at liberty to divulge any indentifying information."

"This is really important. I don't know what to do except to ask for your help. Maybe there is something in the file that you can divulge. Would you please try for me?"

"Okay," she said reluctantly. I'm swamped this time of year, but I'll see what I can do?"

"Thank you Mrs. Kaplan. I appreciate your help with this urgent matter. Would you please call me as soon as you review my file? Here's my phone number," Ellen said handing over a piece of paper with her name and number. "Please call me."

Later that week, Ellen called Rabbi Golden as promised.

"Rabbi Golden, I know that Noah briefly spoke to you last week, but I have a situation and I find that I need your consul."

Of course, how can I help you?"

"Rabbi. I am adopted."

"I think I did know that."

"Well…," she paused organizing her thoughts, then took a deep breath and continued, "I think you met Daniel on Simchat Torah (the Jewish holiday in autumn celebrating the conclusion of the Torah reading cycle) when he happened to be in town helping with youth programming."

"Yes. Such a nice boy. He has a rather dry sense of humor as I recall."

"Yes, true, true. Rabbi, he and Rachel have gotten serious and they plan to get engaged in a few months."

"That's wonderful news!"

"Thank you. We are delighted! He's a truly special boy and it's very exciting. But my problem is this. A few days ago, Rachel happened to mention to Daniel that I was adopted. So he asked her, curiously and innocently, how I know that I'm Jewish. Rachel told him I had always known, which is completely truthful, but later she called Noah and asked him exactly how I knew. Of course, the ramifications are very clear. How does she know that she is Jewish? On the brink of the engagement, this is suddenly very important as it should be," expressed Ellen.

"Ellen, do you know anything about your birth mother."

"Very little. I know that I was adopted through the Jewish Adoption Center. So, before Rachel was born I went to JAC and filed for a report of non-identifying information. This is the information that they can give you from your file that withholds anything that will help you to identify the birth parents. I have a document from JAC with that information. I've kept it in our safe deposit box since shortly after Rachel's birth."

"What specifically did it say?"

"It states that she was a single Jewish woman, who had a Bat Mitzvah. Is that enough to know?" Ellen asked hopefully.

"I don't believe that would be considered enough proof. Is there a way to find out more about your mother?"

"I think it will be very hard. The report also said that she was an only child and her mother died when she was only seven and her father when she was eighteen. She has probably married and changed her name and with no siblings or parents with the same last name, I believe it will be nearly impossible to find her."

"The way that Jewish law (halacha) works in this case, is that one looks to their mother and their grandmother before them to determine their status as a Jew. The information is usually readily available because family members are known to each other. I believe we need more real information. I know of a few rabbis who deal specifically with adoption cases. I'll speak to them and find out exactly what options there are. Let's talk again in a few days. Is that okay with you, Ellen?"

"To be honest, I'm very overwhelmed by this. Time is of the essence and I don't know how I'll get more specifics. Thank you rabbi. Yes. I'll call you later in the week."

Ellen was disappointed. How in the world was she going to find proof and fast? Rabbi Golden would look into it and she was sure that he would be of great help, but she knew that more proof was needed than a document written by an unknown social worker over 40 years before. Times were different than when she was married. Not too many years ago, the whole "Who is a Jew?" issue wreaked havoc in Israel, the times demanded more and she knew she had to find more – but how?

After she hung up with Rabbi Golden, the phone immediately rang. It was Rachel. Ellen braced herself for the inevitable question. "Hi honey, how are you?"

"I'm good Mom, and you?

"Fine. What's up?" Ellen asked even though she dreaded the inevitable response.

"Did you find out any information yet about the adoption thing?"

"Rachel, I'm truly working on it. I just had a phone conversation with Rabbi Golden. He thinks I may need to get more concrete proof. I'm still waiting for the person from the Jewish Adoption Center to get back to me. I told her it was urgent."

"Mom, it's really important," Rachel persisted.

"I understand honey. I'll let you know as soon as I figure something out."

"Okay Mom. I have to go. Please let me know as soon as you know anything."

"Of course. Bye Rachel. Have a good day." Ellen hung up. She passed the mirror in the living room as she went to hang up the phone. As she looked in the mirror, she didn't like the strain she saw in her face. Rachel didn't mean to push, yet pushed is how Ellen felt. Pushed into finding information she never truly wanted, Ellen found herself driven to find a quick solution so she could move past this issue. She wanted to scream and scream with frustration. Instead, she picked up the phone and dialed her friend Wendy. She needed to vent.

On tenterhooks, Ellen waited a full week hoping to hear news from Mrs. Kaplan. Lying on her bed with a cold compress on her brow, she carefully dialed the adoption office. When Mrs. Kaplan answered on the fourth ring, Ellen plowed ahead.

"Mrs. Kaplan, it's Ellen Sachs again. How are you today?"

"Fine, Mrs. Sachs. What can I do for you?"

"I just wanted to check on my file and see if you've made any progress."

"No. Mrs. Sachs. I am swamped here as I told you. I'm the only one that handles adoption information."

"I understand Mrs. Kaplan, but it has already been a week. I truly don't want to be a pest, but my daughter wants to get engaged soon and I need to know if there is anything else in the file that can be gleaned."

"Mrs. Sachs, are you actually sure you were adopted through JAC? To be honest, I looked around yesterday for your file and didn't find anything."

"What do you mean? You couldn't find my file. I know for sure that I was adopted through your agency, because I have a report from just before Rachel's birth, which would be around late 1986, written by a woman who worked at JAC. That's the office in which I filed and picked up the report." Ellen said as her agitation level rose exponentially.

"You say you have a report from this office?"

"Yes. Dated 1986."

"Mrs. Sachs, could you bring me a copy? It may help me locate your file."

Ellen was furious. "Mrs. Kaplan," she said trying not to scream, "I will be there within a half hour. Will you be there at that time?"

"Yes. I'll be here."

"Good. See you then," Ellen said through gritted teeth. Ellen hung up and then she did scream. She grabbed her safe deposit box key, her jacket and pocketbook, pulled out her car keys and ran out the door. She grumbled as she drove the short distance to the bank where she waited impatiently for the bank officer to notice her standing by the safe entrance – standard procedure at her bank. She gathered the report from the safe deposit box, then waited again for the bank officer to return, check the room where she had opened her box, and finally stow the box back in its slot in the vault. Ellen hoped she hadn't been rude through the process, so she took an extra moment to truly thank the bank officer. With proof in her hand, she drove to the JAC building. Twenty-five short minutes from the time of their phone conversation, Ellen was ushered into Mrs. Kaplan's office.

"That was certainly fast Mrs. Sachs," Mrs. Kaplan said surprised to see Ellen so quickly.

"Yes. Well, this situation is urgent for me, Mrs. Kaplan."

Taking the letter from Ellen's outstretched hand Mrs. Kaplan said, "I'll make a copy of your report, and then we can talk about it."

"Fine," Ellen replied as she sank heavily into a chair and began to catch her breath.

Mrs. Kaplan returned a few minutes later with the copy in her hand. "Here is your original. I don't want anything to happen to it."

"Thank you. I'll return it to the safe deposit box as soon as possible just in case something comes up again."

Looking over the report, Mrs. Kaplan assured Ellen, "You're right. This is certainly from our agency, and I know the woman who made the report."

"Does she still work here?"

"Unfortunately, no. She hasn't worked here in years."

"Do you think you can locate my file more readily with this?"

"Yes. I believe so."

"Is there any way that you can rush the review process and look it over quickly? As I have said before, I'm not trying to be a pest. The information is urgent. Any information on my grandmother or my mother's heritage may really help me."

"As I already told you, it's a remote possibility that I will find any information that will solve your problem, but I will see what I can do when I can."

Reluctantly Ellen replied, "Thank you Mrs. Kaplan. I appreciate your help."

Ellen was becoming convinced that this was a dead end. Possibly some information could be uncovered during a full search process, but there was simply not enough time to start that.

Ellen waited a few more days and then called Rabbi Golden at his office to find out if he had any new information.

"Ellen, I did some research and spoke to the leading authority on adoption issues, Rabbi Woodberg. He is located in New York which may be helpful to Rachel since she is in school in the city. Just as I thought, he does not feel that the report from the Jewish Adoption Center is sufficient as proof. He said we must find more compelling factual documentation or a relative that can attest to the Jewish identity of your mother as well as her mother, your grandmother.

"Rabbi, I don't see how this will be possible. I've gotten no closer to finding my mother's identity. I have no idea what to do!"

"There is another option available and Rabbi Woodberg said often people must go this route, a conversion of doubt."

"What is a conversion of doubt? I've never heard of such a thing."

"It's a regular conversion process done for individuals who are knowledgeable and practicing their Judaism but who need to remove any doubt as to their Jewishness. In your case and for the girls, it would involve going to a mikvah (ritual bath filled with pure rain water) and immersing in the mikvah with three witnesses present. You would not be required to follow the usual stringent guidelines of study and preparation as in a regular conversion."

"Oh. Three women witnesses?" Ellen asked hopefully, fully realizing that women in Orthodox Judaism are not usually allowed to be witnesses for ritual activities.

"No. They must be male witnesses. But Ellen, please understand that the men cannot see anything. They will be behind a screen and will only turn to look once you are safely underwater and the mikvah lady who will help you perform the proper procedures will cue them on this."

Ellen knew from experience that mikvah immersion regularly done by married women was a very private, spiritual practice in which one carefully prepares their body by cleaning, shampooing, trimming nails, removing any polish, even going so far as to make sure not a hair has fallen onto the skin. A woman, trained in examining for details, modestly checks over the fully unclothed woman who is there to immerse, and then gives the signal to begin. Once a person has completed her immersion, the mikvah lady helps her quickly back into her robe, and then she is pronounced spiritually clean.

"Rabbi, I want to get this straight," Ellen faltered, "are you saying that my unmarried daughters, who have never been to the mikvah before, will need to do their first immersion with men present?"

"Yes. That is how it's done, but the men will only view your daughters after they are under and only to make sure that they are under the water. They will not see anything untoward."

"I hear what you're saying, but this is not okay with me," Ellen said miserably. "I'll have to speak to the girls. Is there anything else I need to know about this conversion of doubt?" she asked apprehensively.

"There is one more important point. Is Daniel a Kohain?"

Racking her brain, Ellen considered what being a Kohain could have to do with this discussion. She knew that in Judaism the Jewish identity is passed by the mother, but the tribal line of Kohain, Levi or Yisrael is passed down through the father. The Kohainim (Kohain in the plural) are the descendants of the high priests of Israel and as such they have certain special requirements that are uniquely theirs. For example, the Kohainim are not allowed to be near a dead body or to attend to a dead body. "No, he's a Levi," Ellen answered.

Rabbi Golden continued," Kohainim are not allowed to marry converts. This is considered a conversion, and the girls will not be able to marry a boy who is a Kohain. For Rachel, that won't be an issue."

"But it could be for Lily and Jill," Ellen said tears brimming in her eyes. "What if they fall in love with boys that are Kohainim? This is so upsetting!"

"The numbers are in their favor, though. Most people are Yisrael, followed by Levi. It's a small percentage of the population that are Kohainim."

"But it easily could happen. I don't know, rabbi. This is difficult to take in."

"I know, but I am sure everything will work out. Rabbi Woodberg said he would gladly speak to you or

Rachel and help to expedite things. You could all do the conversion in New York together."

"Lily just went back to Israel. The teacher's strike is finally over and her classes just began last week." Ellen said sadly, "She waited here for months. I don't know, rabbi, I'll have to speak to the girls and Noah and see what to do. Thank you so much. I'll be in touch soon."

"I'm so sorry that you must face this difficulty, but I'm sure it will be good to get things resolved one way or the other."

Ellen had been roaming through the house as she spoke to the rabbi. As she hung up, she slumped on the steps and cried tears of total frustration. Miserably, she contemplated her meager options.

Shortly after, the phone rang and it was Rachel.

"Did you find out anything about the adoption?" Rachel asked moments into the conversation.

"Nothing definitive. I did speak to Rabbi Golden and he said we could all do a conversion of doubt. Since we are already practicing, we would only need to go to the mikvah."

"How soon can we do it?"

"Oh Rachel, there is more to it. Three men will need to be in a screened area adjacent to the mikvah in order to be witnesses. They will be told when to look and will only see once we are completely submerged, but they will still be present."

"That doesn't sound so bad. Can we do it next week?"

"It also means that it's a conversion, a real conversion. You and I are okay, because Daniel and Dad are not Kohanim, but Lily and Jill may have problems. A Kohain won't be allowed to marry them."

"Then maybe they should wait and see what you can find out. Maybe I should do it more quickly. I really need this resolved."

"Yes. I hear you. Hang in there a bit longer. According to Rabbi Golden, Rabbi Woodberg in New York has helped many people with this issue. He said we could come there and he would set it up. Let me find out more details and get back to you."

Later that day, Ellen received an unsettling call from Mrs. Kaplan at the Jewish Adoption Center.

"Mrs. Sachs," Mrs. Kaplan said, "I felt I needed to call you today with an unfortunate development."

"What development?"

"We seem to have lost your file. I have found an indication that it did exist in the form of a card with your biological mother's name, but we've been unable to locate your file."

"You've lost my file!" Ellen cried in anguish. "Have you truly lost the only record of my past?"

"I'm sorry, but it seems that is the case."

"I cannot believe this! What will I do?" Ellen asked in total disbelief. "Can you at least tell me the name on the card you found?"

"I'm not at liberty to do that, but I will tell you that it is a very common Jewish name."

"I don't know what to say, Mrs. Kaplan, I'm truly at a loss here."

"Mrs. Sachs, I'm very sorry to bring you such news."

Chapter Twenty-Six

Noah arrived home from work and found Ellen sitting on the living room sofa, a worried frown creasing her face.

"Ellen, what's up buttercup?"

"What – oh hi Noah," Ellen said suddenly laughing. "I have never heard you call me that before."

"And I have never seen you consistently so sad. It just came to me. Let's go out for dinner and put the whole adoption thing aside for a bit."

"I was just thinking about the conversion of doubt. What if we have to go that route?"

"Then we will. The girls will be okay with it."

"I'm not so sure."

"I know you are uncomfortable with the idea, but most converts do the same thing. Their first time in the mikvah is done with witnesses. People do this all the time without problem."

"I am sure they do, but these are not just people. These are our daughters," Ellen said placing her hands over her heart emphasizing her words. "I don't want them to be traumatized. It's also the whole Kohain issue. What will Lily and Jill do if they want to marry Kohainim one day?"

"I don't know, but we are not there yet. Let's go out – I'm hungry and I want to eat a nice dinner with my beautiful wife without a frown on her face," he said as he reached down and planted a teasing kiss on her lips. "Let's go for Chinese. That will cheer you up. Come on," he said pulling her up from the sofa and leading her toward the door.

"Wait a minute. I have to at least fix my makeup," she said with a smile. "I'm lucky I have you, you know."

"I know. I know," he said taking off an imaginary hat and brandishing it for her in his outstretched hand. "Hurry up, buttercup."

***

The following Monday morning, Ellen headed off to work at the Office of Vital Events. The heritage issue weighed so heavily on her, she could barely get herself dressed and ready in time. Before she had even gotten her coat off, Ellen saw Kelly who was headed to the vault area.

"Hi Kelly," Ellen called out as she followed Kelly into the vault.

"Hi Ellen," How are you today?"

"Fine. Fine. And you? How is your husband feeling? I know he has been a bit under the weather?"

"Thanks for asking. He's a bit better."

"Kelly, I know I have asked you before, but I am back to the adoption thing."

"You are a little early this year aren't you?" Kelly replied with a smile.

"Ha ha," Ellen said. It was a running joke that Ellen got worked up a bit about the adoption issue around her birthday in January. Ellen had plopped down in Kelly's office for an adoption chat every January for the last four or five years. Three years in a row Kelly had listened and then given Ellen the brochure for the Mutual Consent Voluntary Adoption Registry, a registry created in 1996 by the State Legislature in which adoptees, birth parents and birth siblings chose to place their names in the registry in the hopes that the registry staff would find a match when comparing their information with those of other registrants. The fee was a nominal $25, and Ellen went as far the third time as to call the number provided in the brochure. She had the form sent to her and had even filled it out, but she had not sent it. Something held her back, and a few months ago she had noticed the filled out form under some papers in her office. At the time, she had simply thrown the paper out, realizing that her actions were a decision in themselves, a decision that clearly meant she was not ready to move forward in a search.

"Kelly, I never did register on the Mutual Consent Voluntary Adoption Registry, and I had no luck with either the county or city courts opening my file," Ellen began.

"I know. It's very strange about the courts. I would've thought that the city court would have your record by what you had told me and know to be true."

"The decision to search has changed. I suddenly find that I need to know some things about my birth mother and I need the information very fast."

"Is something wrong?"

Ellen was in a quandary. Kelly was not Jewish and Ellen was not sure how to explain the need to prove one's Jewish identity. She, herself, was not truly on board with the need to find proof, yet she struggled daily with the unfairness and inequity of her situation. She decided to minimize the Jewish thing and work on the medical necessity angle. Ellen did feel strongly that she should get an update on medical issues in the family. What if the kids were to need something from a relative and no one on Noah's side matched? In fact, her friend Pam was scheduled to have a kidney transplant that very week. Pam's brother had abused his own system and his kidneys were failing. His only chance was a transplant, and Pam was the perfect match. Ellen had listened as Pam confided her feelings of anger and responsibility toward her brother, finally deciding that she had no real choice and would do the amazing kindness of giving up one of her own kidneys – and compromising her own life, for her brother. This weighed heavily on Ellen's mind as well. So, she plowed ahead, "I must find out if there are any medical issues in the family. I need the answers soon before my daughter Rachel gets married."

"That's wonderful. Is she engaged yet?"

"Not yet. She and Daniel are very close. This has to be resolved first."

"Ellen, I really don't know what I can do. I'm sympathetic but rules are rules and I'm bound by the state laws that govern to whom and when information may be released."

"Of course. I don't want you to do anything that's not allowed, but it's so very hard for me. I can't ask my adopted parents anything that will shed light on this."

"Why not? Are they unwilling to share information with you."

"Kelly, they have both been deceased for years. My father since I was fifteen and my mother since the year you met me in 1996. I'm pretty sure that I've mentioned this before."

"Really? Oh. I'm sorry." Kelly paused deep in thought and then coming to a conclusion she brightened, "You know what Ellen?"

"What?"

"I can open your file. With both your parents deceased, I can open it and look."

"Seriously?" Ellen stammered. "Are you really serious? What do I need to do?" How soon can we get it?"

"Yes. I'm serious. We can open it," Kelly replied laughing at Ellen's lightning fast jump from if to what to when. "Fill out an application for your birth certificate and include a check for $12. That's all you need to do. I will send for the file from the archives. We need to be a bit patient, because it takes up to a week to get here."

"Why does it take a week?"

"Things aren't automated there. Someone has to manually find the file in a stack of boxes and then send it by FedEx to this office from the office in Annapolis. I'll call and see if they can rush it a bit."

"That would be amazing. I'll be in your office in five minutes or less with the application," Ellen replied excitedly. And she was. With a flourish, Ellen signed the application for her REAL birth certificate and ceremoniously handed over the $12 fee. Could this truly be happening? Ellen thought, astonished by the sudden development.

Chapter Twenty-Seven

November 16, 2007

Ellen, dressed all in black, stealthily searched through the boxes at the archives. She and Kelly had outwitted the security guard and slipped unseen into the main storage area. With Kelly as the lookout, Ellen ran up and down the rows of boxes stored in pullout containers from floor to ceiling noting the years labeled on the top of each row. Finally, she came to 1963.

Kelly whispered, "Lights out," and Ellen quickly extinguished her flashlight as footsteps passed the doorway.

"All clear," Kelly whispered a few moments later. Ellen shined her light down the row of boxes and found the one labeled January 1963 – Adoptions. As quietly as she could, she moved the ladder they had found by the entrance to the room over to the stack. Climbing up the ladder, Ellen reached the box near the top. Carefully, she pulled open the box and forced herself to methodically start at the beginning as she moved through the yellow taped files until she found the one labeled: BRENNER-ELLEN – January 17, 1963. She pulled out the file and quietly closed the box pushing it back into its slot.

"Lights out," Kelly called just above a whisper again. Ellen turned off her flashlight and held tight to the ladder waiting. "All clear," Kelly's voice floated up again. Ellen flashed her light on the file, carefully opened the taped edge and rummaged through the contents. Finding her original birth certificate, she leaned heavily against the ladder as she fumbled in her jacket pocket for her digital camera. She took several pictures of the certificate and reviewed them in the viewfinder. Placing the certificate back in the file and then in the box, she slid the box home again and made her way down the ladder.

With rapid, light steps she made her way to Kelly. "I got it," Ellen whispered just as the guard turned his gaze into the startled faces of Ellen and Kelly.

Ellen awoke that Friday confused and shaken. I am losing it, she thought as she shook off the dream. The wait for the file to come from the archives was all-consuming, while the minutes in their excruciating slowness practically ticked backward like a clock with a low battery. Unable to adequately convey the enormity of the situation even to those closest to her, Ellen struggled isolated and alone. This was a search of necessity, not one of choice, therefore Ellen was powerless to protect herself. The information soon to be gleaned would change her. She was sure of that. What she didn't know and what was keeping her on tenterhooks, was how much and in what way she would be changed.

Friday was Ellen's day off of work. Guests had been invited weeks before, so she spent the morning inefficiently preparing for a festive Sabbath meal. Around noon, her anxiety peaked and Ellen simply couldn't wait anymore, so she drove the short distance to her office.

"The delivery company has not made its drop off today," Kelly said when Ellen caught up to her in the hallway. "They should be here by noon."

Looking at the analog office-issue clock a few feet above Kelly's head, Ellen noticed that it was already a bit after eleven. With herculean restraint, Ellen refrained from stomping her feet like a petulant child, forced a small smile and replied, "Okay. I think I'll hang around the mall. I'll be back by twelve."

The Vital Events office had been moved to a local mall ten years prior when a state bigwig had decided that it would be a great idea for customers to order their certificates and then shop while the certificates were prepared. In reality, long lines of people requesting certificates flowed out into the mall and the line often extended the distance of two or three store lengths. The waiting room was consistently packed as customers waited for their certificates. Possibly the mall traffic increased, but Ellen noticed that most people came for their certificates, waited at the office for the certificates and then headed out. Regardless, Ellen used the mall tactic on that very day to distract her during the endless wait.

Moments after twelve, Ellen rushed back to the office and headed directly to Kelly's office.

"It's here!" Kelly exclaimed waving papers in the air as she came up behind Ellen outside her door. "Come into my office," she said almost pushing Ellen into the office in her own excitement. "I had a few minutes after it arrived to make copies for you. I have your birth certificate and I found your mother's birth certificate too! She was also born in Maryland."

"Really?" Ellen squeaked as she positioned herself by the edge of Kelly's desk. "I'm so nervous!"

"Here is your birth certificate," Kelly said as she ceremoniously placed the single-page copy on the desk in front of Ellen.

Immediately, Ellen's heart rate increased exponentially. Wiping her instantly drenched palms on her skirt, she took a deep breath, swept the room once with her eyes, glanced at Kelly's eager face and then finally down at the remarkable paper that lay in front of her. The words took a moment to come into focus and then there it was - her mother's actual name – Jo Engle. Could it be, could it be? Ellen thought in staccato. "Could it be this easy?" Ellen said the sound muffled beneath her hands that had flown to her face covering her mouth.

"What's wrong?"

"No," Ellen said bringing her hands back down to the desktop and gripping the paper. "Nothing's wrong, something may be very right! My mother's last name is Engle. My husband and I know so many people named Engle, some of our closest friends in fact," Ellen burst out. "Could it be the same family? This is unbelievable…. Maybe I will be able to solve my problem," Ellen mumbled. Mrs. Kaplan had been right, Ellen thought, it was a familiar name in the community. Reading further, Ellen exclaimed, "I was given a name at birth. I didn't think I had. My name was – Louisa Engle. Wow!" She said with shining eyes. "This is so amazing!"

"I'm really happy for you, Ellen," Kelly said rounding the desk and giving Ellen a big hug. Moving back behind her desk, she placed a second page in front of Ellen. "I found some more information for you. From your mother's certificate, I found out the names of your grandparents as well. Your grandfather was William and your grandmother Louisa."

"Oh my goodness. So much information so fast! I don't know what to say. I can't thank you enough, Kelly. Really I can't." Reading further, Ellen noticed, "Look, it says I was born at Forest Hospital and on the 17th!" Ellen gasped. Remembering the fact, that it was common practice to change adoptees birth dates on their certificates by a day or two, she was ecstatic to realize that she had indeed known the correct birth date all along. "I always thought I was born at Centennial Hospital," Ellen continued the revelations. "This is amazing! It means so much to have my real birth certificate. I can't tell you how much!" Pausing and almost embarrassed, Ellen asked, "Hey Kelly, now that I have my mother's name, is it too greedy to want my father's as well? The certificate just states that the patient prefers not to give this information."

"I see. Well, that happens a lot. Mothers aren't forced to include the paternity information if they don't want to. I think it's perfectly understandable that you would want to know your father's name as well. It isn't greedy at all."

"Thanks." Rebounding quickly, Ellen said while rising, "Kelly, thanks so very much! Thanks for the information and the encouragement. I have to go call Noah and then I have some important friends to call. This is insane! I'll fill you in on Monday!" She exclaimed with a wave as she excitedly hurried out."

"Good luck, Ellen," Kelly said smiling as she watched her go.

Ellen nearly ran to her car. Whipping out her cell phone, she dialed Noah. In one breath she unloaded, "Noah, you will never guess. My file arrived and I have a copy of my real birth certificate. My mother's name is Jo Engle. ENGLE!" Then more slowly, "Do you think I could actually be related to Stan and Rebecca and Meyer and Eve and everyone else?"

"Whoa, I don't know Ellen. That's amazing! Where are you?"

"Just outside my office."

"Do me a favor and drive home carefully. Take your time," he cautioned. "We'll talk about all this when I get home."

"Do you think I should call Stan right now? Do you have his number at work?"

"Go home first. It'll wait for a minute. I have to go, but drive carefully. I'll be home in a few hours."

Ellen couldn't wait, so she called her friends Stan and Melinda. No answer. Then she called Stan's sister Rebecca. Again, no answer. Of course no one is home at 1:00 on a Friday afternoon, she thought. Before she knew it, Ellen had driven the short seven minute ride home and was pulling into her driveway. Lucky the car knows the way, she thought.

As she pulled her jacket off, Ellen figured out who to call, Stan's parents. The senior Engles knew her and Noah well. Noah had grown up with Stan and they had been friends forever. Reflecting back, Ellen couldn't pinpoint when she had first met Stan, but she knew it was at least 25 years. Frantically, she ran around the house looking for a phone and the community phone book. As she dialed Mr. and Mrs. Engle, she wondered what she would say. Mrs. Engle answered the call on the third ring.

After quick pleasantries were exchanged Ellen got to the point. "Mrs. Engle," she asked, "does Mr. Engle have a relative named Jo?"

"Yes dear. I believe he does," replied Mrs. Engle.

"Would she be about 60 now?"

"Yes. That would be about right. She is Milton's first cousin, but she's a bit younger."

"Do you know where she lives?"

"No. I don't think so. I haven't seen her in years, but Milton would be the best person to ask. Ellen, what's up hon?" Mrs. Engle asked with her pronounced Baltimore accent.

Worried that Mrs. Engle may be shocked by the news and realizing that she was not a young woman, Ellen coaxed, "Mrs. Engle, would you sit down please before I continue?"

"This sounds serious. Okay."

"Are you sitting?"

"Yes, hon. I am."

"Okay. I don't want to frighten you. I think you know I'm adopted."

"Yes. I did know that."

"Well, I just saw a copy of my real birth certificate and my biological mother is named Jo Engle."

"Oh my my, that's news."

"Yes. It really is. You know what? We could be related."

"That would be wonderful dear, but I think you will need to check with Milton. He keeps a genealogy of everyone in the family. He should be able to help you."

"Where is he? May I speak to him?"

"He isn't here right now. He went to the bagel store for lunch, but I'll have him call you right away when he gets back."

"Thank you so much. Are you okay with this? I haven't shocked you have I?" Ellen asked with genuine concern. The news was overwhelming for her, but she had no idea how others would feel.

"I'm just fine. This is fascinating. I'll tell Milton."

It had only been an hour and Ellen felt her life had shifted with each new disclosure. Pacing the living/dining room combination, she repeatedly plumped the pillows on the two taupe leather sofas set at right angles to each other. Momentarily finding a more productive focus, she set the table in the dining room with fine china and glassware in festive mode for the upcoming Sabbath meal. She cringed at the idea of entertaining guests that evening and having to make and follow conversation when she could barely organize her thoughts. She finished up the final food preparation tasks and then paced some more, waiting for Milton Engle to return home from the bagel shop and call her. Three separate times in the long two hour wait, she retrieved her car keys from her pocketbook and went to the door planning to go to the bagel store and find him. Shaking her head at her impatience, she stopped herself each time.

Finally, the phone rang and Ellen pounced on it. Hannah Engle had filled Milton in on the news. He had instantly retrieved his most recent copy of the family genealogy chart and dialed Ellen's number.

Relieved to hear his voice, Ellen shortened the pleasantries and began, "Hello, Mr. Engle, thanks so much for calling back. I'm trying to find my biological mother."

"Hannah told me. I hope I can be of help."

"Let's see if my information matches. Were your cousin Jo's parents William and Louisa Engle?

"Yes. They were. I knew William well. My twin brother and I worked in his store for years. He was a gem of a man."

"Wow," Ellen said hands flying to her rapidly beating heart center. "Did you know Louisa?"

"Yes, I did although not as well. She was sick and died young as I recall."

"That matches with my information. Did you know Jo also?" She said, holding her breath.

"Of course. She's my first cousin. She is a bit younger than me and we didn't see her often, but I do remember her as a quiet, pretty girl."

"Do you think she would be around 64 now?"

"Hmmm," Milton murmured thinking, "I have my chart right here. She was born in July, 1943 and this is November, 2007. Yes, she would be exactly 64, though I haven't seen her in years. Ellen, on my chart I see that Jo has two daughters listed. You don't seem to be on the list."

"Mr. Engle, I wouldn't be on the list," Ellen said with stunned understanding. After a brief moment, she continued poignantly, "I am the one that didn't make it to the list."

"I guess that would be so," he said pausing. "On the chart, the two daughters are Leanne Young and Mandy Romano. I suppose they are your half-sisters."

"Half sisters," Ellen mimicked, "I really hadn't prepared myself for siblings." Thinking back, Ellen realized that she hadn't thought about the possibility of siblings in years and years, not since she was in elementary school. Cautiously Ellen put the notion forth, "I know this is incredible, but it sounds like your cousin really is my biological mother." Holding her breath, Ellen waited for his reaction.

"I think so too. All the facts work. Life truly is a wonder. Welcome to the family, Ellen!" He said and Ellen felt his warmth emanate through the phone connection.

"Oh," she said with gratitude, "thank you thank you. I'm really excited and honored!"

"You're welcome. I think we have a lot to discuss, but it is getting close to the Sabbath. I would love to show you the genealogy chart, and I think I may be able to find a few pictures of Jo. Why don't you and Noah come over tomorrow night and we'll look it all over?"

"That sounds perfect. Pictures. I wonder if I look like her. Is this really happening?" She wondered aloud. "Thanks so much again, Mr. Engle. We will be over by 9:00. Have a good Sabbath. Send my best to Mrs. Engle. Is she all right with all this? I didn't startle her too much, did I?" Ellen added with concern.

"No, no. She is fine. Not to worry. We will see you tomorrow."

Stunned, Ellen pressed the off button on the phone. She slowly placed the phone on the hall table and as she did she looked up and glimpsed herself in the hallway mirror. Bending close toward the mirror, she methodically examined her appearance. She saw the same brown eyes flecked with hazel, the same dark brown almost black hair, the same fair complexion, but she realized she was different; the tendrils of a new reality were seeping into her core. She was part of another family, she had people who were related and shared blood relationships – she had ROOTS! Ellen came from somewhere and that somewhere was coming into view – no longer a blank vision. With the birth of their three children, Ellen and Noah had actualized Ellen's unconscious need for physical connection with others, sharing of DNA, sharing of physical traits and characteristics. This was different. This fulfilled a deep need for a connection to the past, a connection to the line of her descendants. No longer was Ellen the root of her tree. As she stared into the mirror, she virtually felt imaginary shoots sprout beneath her connecting her to past generations. Ellen momentarily wondered about the men and women who constituted her new lineage which in Judaism is referred to as yichus, the idea that if your predecessors have brought honor to the family through their accomplishments in life, the hope will be that the apple would not fall far from the tree. The fruit will have the potential to be even stronger than the branch, therefore giving honor to the offspring.

Pulling herself from her musings, Ellen called Rachel. Catching her at a quiet moment in her dorm room in downtown Manhattan, Ellen hurriedly recounted the events of the day.

"Mom, does this mean we don't need to do the conversion of doubt?" Rachel said in confusion leaning back on her bed, her back against the wall as she looked around the alcove which housed her bed and dresser.

"Yes. I think so. I will check with Rabbi Golden, but I think we should be able to get some of the

Engles to vouch for Jo's Jewish identity. I will let you know as soon as I can."

"Mom, I need to know for sure soon," Rachel reminded.

Ellen understood that Rachel wasn't vested in the search and the consequences of uncovering biological connections. Her only interest was the expedited determination of her Jewishness, but she included, "Rachel, this means also that you and Bengy are cousins of some sort." Bengy was Stan and Melinda's oldest son and a good friend of Rachel's. They had been in class together all the way from kindergarten through high school. Of course Rachel was now cousins with Stan's and Rebecca's and Eve's and Meyer's kids as well. All lived close by in their tight-knit community and all had attended the Jewish Day school that the four families, along with many others, had helped to start fifteen years before.

"That is weird, Mom."

"I know. I'll find out more and let you know as soon as possible."

"Was Mr. Engle really sure about all this?"

"All the information I have gathered, the non-identifying information from the JAC report and the names and ages from my real birth certificate matched. I think it is extremely unlikely that another Jo Engle could exist who definitely lived in this area, is the correct age and had a mother and father die when she was young at the exact ages listed on the JAC report. Also, Mr. Engle knew Jo, her father and mother, her stepmother. Everything! Although I am clearly still adjusting to the possibility myself, I think we do know for sure," Ellen answered emotionally.

After hanging up with Rachel, Ellen turned her thoughts to their middle daughter, Lily, far away in Israel in another time zone seven hours ahead. It was already the Sabbath in Israel, which meant that Lily would not answer the phone until Saturday after nightfall. Lily had four Engle cousins in her class throughout her years of school. Whereas only one was Rachel's age, four were Lily's age. One of her closest friends in the world was now her cousin as well, and Ellen found this news exciting but possibly unsettling. Worried about her sensitive daughter, Ellen dialed the number in Israel and left a message. Unfortunately, she failed to plan her words and tone carefully enough and all the message seemed to convey at first was something cataclysmic. Hours later, Lily sat trembling as she listened to her mother's taped voice, wondering what disaster had befallen their family. When she finally understood the whole message, Lily was relieved although traumatized by the worry her mother caused, not by the actual import.

Moments later, Jill arrived home from her day at school. Ellen shared the news with her.

"So you see Jill, I think that Stan and Rebecca and Meyer and Eve are all my second cousins, which means that you have a whole bunch of new cousins too."

"That is so cool, Mom. Wow. I love the Engles. They are great! I can't wait to call Alan and tell him."

Alan was Stan and Melinda's youngest son and he was Jill's peer. Stan and Melinda had three boys the same ages as Noah and Ellen's three girls, and the families had shared some wonderful vacations together. The group was quite simpatico, except for the time when Lily was a baby and Ellen had run out of formula leaving Lily to cry nonstop all the way home in the car during one such trip and Stan threatening to never vacation with them again. Jokingly, formula quantities were always considered before subsequent outings.

"Hey Mom, I think you should start calling yourself Lou for Louisa. I think it's catchy."

"Thanks, but I think I'll stick with Ellen for now, though I am glad you approve," Ellen said beaming.

Home from work and changing into his Sabbath clothes, Noah handled the additional news with a mixed reaction. "This is all remarkable Ellen. To think that some of my oldest friends are now relatives. It's hard to wrap my head around. I wonder how they will take it."

"I don't know, Noah. I'm a bit worried about that. It's seems kind of a crazy thing to call your friends and say oh by the way I am your newly found cousin. It's a bizarre situation. That's for sure."

Noah had hit the problem right on. Ellen's most immediate concern was upsetting the family. She didn't want to appear to be nudging in where she was not wanted or needed. On top of everything, this was only one part of the family. She still had half-sisters to contend with and possibly a meeting in the near future with her birth mother. Too much to process, she kept thinking.

Remarkably, Ellen managed to compartmentalize the earth shattering news and her worries long enough to finish her Sabbath preparations and receive her guests.

Chapter Twenty-Eight

November 17, 2007

Ellen awoke with a grunt. Eyes tightly closed, she reached her right arm out and rubbed her fingers along the cool empty sheets, registering the fact that Noah had already left for synagogue. Cobwebby images of a mother she had never known, leftover fragments of her fitful sleep slowly dissipated from her groggy mind. Giving herself a few more minutes before facing the big day, she found her emotions and thoughts alternating between worry about the reception she would receive from the Engle clan and amazement over the revelations of the day before. Swinging her legs over the side of the bed, she vaulted herself to an upright position and hurried to the bathroom. She needed to get a move on.

She turned on the cold water tap full force. As she cupped the water in her hands and splashed it on her face, she felt somewhat revived. I look a mess, she said to herself as she noticed the huge bags under her eyes. Ugh. She grabbed a plush green towel and slowly dried her face, deep in thought. Many of her friends, now family, were members and regular worshippers at the synagogue she and Noah attended. She knew that she would see at least ten or twelve of them in a few hours. Confident that the news had run through the grapevine, she felt an equal mixture of excitement and nervousness.

She entered her small but functional walk-in closet and pulled out five outfits before settling on a tried and true black skirt with an interesting weave design, a white blouse tucked into the skirt and topped off by a teal blue cropped button-down sweater. Black patent leather low-heeled pumps, her go to black small rimmed wool hat and silver jewelry completed the ensemble. Checking herself in the full-length mirror inside the closet, she picked up her glasses and left the bedroom. After setting the lunch meal of chicken, rice, potatoes and string beans on the hot plate to warm while she was in synagogue, Ellen put on her blue pea coat and closed the door. Then, as usual, she checked the lock twice.

The brisk mile-long walk to synagogue felt good, and Ellen used the twenty minutes to convince herself that all would be well. Completely absorbed in her thoughts, she failed to notice her friend Wendy until Wendy appeared beside her.

"Ellen, I've been trying to catch up with you for a block, you didn't even hear me calling," Wendy said breathlessly.

"Oh Wendy, I'm so sorry. I was deep in thought."

"Everything okay?"

"Yes. In fact, I wanted to call you yesterday but ran out of time. I did it! I got my real birth certificate!" Ellen exclaimed.

"That's spectacular! How did you feel?"

"You would ask that," Ellen said, laughing at her friend the social worker. "Actually I was very nervous and excited and terrified at the same time, but the most amazing thing is that my birth name was ENGLE."

"Really? That's incredible. Do you think you are related to all the Engle family we know – the whole mishpacha (family)."

"Yes. I do. I spoke to Milton Engle yesterday and we shared information. Everything matched up perfectly with no glitches. I'm convinced that I am actually a second cousin to Stan and Rebecca and Meyer and Eve. All our grandfathers were brothers; the name of mine was William. Wendy, I'm concerned about everyone's reaction. Do you think they will think it is presumptuous of me to push myself into the family this way?"

"In what way? You didn't ask to be adopted. You are just presenting the facts. Anyway, they love you already – you have nothing to worry about."

"I'm sure you are right," Ellen said, stopping for a moment and looking at Wendy, "but I can't control how nervous I am."

"Hey, what did Noah say? He has been friends with some of them his whole life."

Resuming the pace, Ellen answered, "He is adjusting. He has always been the primary connection. This kind of changes that a bit, but I think everything will ultimately be fine."

"Definitely. This is so exciting! Good for you. You persevered and found the family. Did you tell the girls?"

"I told Rachel and Jill. Jill was thrilled and really supportive. Rachel found it weird, which it is, but at the end of the day I think we may have solved the Jewish issue, which is the whole point right?"

"That's right. That is where this all started. What a relief for you! What did Lily say?"

"I didn't know anything until the Sabbath had already started in Israel. I left her a message. I hope she's okay finding out all by herself."

"She'll be fine. I am sure you will have a nice discussion with her about it tomorrow." Having arrived at the synagogue, Wendy gave Ellen a big hug. "Good luck with the fa-mi-ly," she said with a huge smile.

"Thanks. I'll see you later," Ellen responded laughing as she moved off to her usual seat on the other side of the synagogue.

As the service proceeded, Ellen was moved when Stan got up to lead. With his rich, sweet voice and pitch perfection honed to a true talent during his days with a local band, Ellen had always enjoyed his voice and tunes and the fact that the key he chose was always one she could sing along with easily. Especially touched and proud on this emotional day, she dabbed at her eyes with a tissue she luckily found in her glass case.

When the service ended, Ellen went to the reception hall. Cake and soft drinks were served as the congregants gathered and socialized. Knowing that the Engle group generally came out the far side of the hall, Ellen made her way over, stopping to greet friends and acquaintances on her way. Even though she had been cold during the service, the temperature in synagogue was always set too cold for the women, she was perspiring. While lifting her arm slightly to assure herself that there was not a sweat stain under her arm, suddenly, she found herself enveloped in a big hug as Melinda cried, "Ellen, what incredible news! We are all so thrilled!"

Laughing, Ellen said, "Mel, me too. The whole thing is surreal. I cannot believe that we're actually related now!"

The celebration escalated as Stan and his sister Rebecca followed by Meyer and his wife Michelle approached with big smiles lighting their faces. Reaching around Melinda for a hug with Ellen, Rebecca exclaimed, "Great news! I already told Rena and she can't wait to speak to Lily. Cousins. We are all cousins!"

"Welcome to the family, cuz," Stan said with a wink and a grin.

"We were so happy to hear the news," Michelle and Meyer chimed together, laughing.

"WOW, thanks Stan, thanks everyone!" Ellen exclaimed looking into each smiling face.

"Tell us all the details," Michelle prompted, "it was so close to the Sabbath and we only got the gist. How did this all come about?"

Out of the corner of Ellen's eye, she smiled as she saw her beautiful youngest daughter, Jill, caught up in a huge hug with Ayelet, one of Meyer and Michelle's two children. The two were surrounded by the younger generation of newly found cousins. The group was laughing and talking just as excitedly as the adults. Animatedly, Ellen relayed all the details and revelations that she had found so far.

As other congregants stopped by, asking questions and joining in the excitement, Ellen looked around for Noah. Searching around the hall with her eyes, she finally found him by the doorway, his face a mix of emotions as he leaned against the doorframe and watched the two converging groups surrounding Ellen and Jill. Ellen motioned to him. Please come over. I need you by my side, she thought. Answering her silent plea, Noah came forward and joined the commotion.

Stan slapped him on the back. "Well old buddy, I guess now we're stuck with each other."

"Yeah. I guess so," Noah answered cheerfully.

Exhilarated by the family meeting, Ellen, Noah and Jill were among the last to leave the reception hall. "That was fun!" Jill exclaimed as they walked home. "Everyone is so excited. What about you, Lou?"

Amused Ellen replied, "It really was fun. Everyone was incredibly understanding and genuinely happy. I'm relieved. Truth be told, I was a bit worried."

Following a brief lunch, Ellen went to make a visit to her friend Pam, who was recovering from a life saving kidney donation operation. While ensconced on the comfortable black leather sofas in Pam's den, Ellen recounted the events of the past two days to her friend, and at Pam's enthusiastic encouragement subsequently to each visitor that came to cheer her friend. At each retelling, Ellen realized the story became more concrete and real to her. The retelling was therapeutic for Ellen and a great diversion for Pam.

Evening came quickly. Ellen and Noah rang the doorbell at the Engle home promptly at 9:00pm.

"Come in, come in. I found some pictures," Mr. Engle dressed in comfortable gray slacks and a white polo shirt said as he opened the door for the couple.

"Hannah, look. Don't you think Ellen looks a great deal like Jo?"

"Hello Ellen, hello Noah," Mrs. Engle said. With a jovial smile on her pleasantly round face she said, "Let me put the picture closer to the light." Glancing from picture to Ellen and back again, she replied. "Yes, I do indeed. There is definitely a resemblance."

Retrieving the picture from Mrs. Engle's outstretched hand, Ellen showed it to Noah. "What do you think?"

Also looking from the picture of Jo at the age of 18 or so and back to Ellen, "I think maybe a bit," Noah answered hesitantly.

Looking deeply for the first time at the image of her mother, Ellen was sadly unmoved. She had thought that she would see much more of a resemblance but more importantly that she would feel some unidentified connection instantly. When she did not, she moved toward a mirror she saw on the wall. Looking deeply into it and then to the picture, she simply saw a young woman with dark hair and eyes, square facial shape - all of which she possessed herself as well - but she thought the resemblance ended there. The woman-girl in the picture was of a bigger build, her eyes slightly farther apart, her nose wider and her lips fuller. Ellen didn't see herself in the picture, although both Mr. and Mrs. Engle enthusiastically disagreed.

"I found the phone number for one of your half-sisters, Mandy Romano," Mr. Engle said as he handed Ellen a yellow slip of paper with the name and number written on it.

"How did you find the number? Did one of the relatives have it?" Ellen asked.

"I don't know if any do, but I looked it up on the Internet. It only took a few minutes. Luckily, she hasn't changed her last name."

"You found it so fast. That's incredible. Thank you so much."

Moving toward a table in the corner of the room, Mr. Engle motioned the group over. "Here is the genealogy chart I have been keeping up. On this level," he said indicating a row of names connected by straight lines, "your grandfather's level there were twelve children although two died young. Here is your branch with William married to Louisa and then Jo. According to the chart Jo married a man named George Millstein and they had two children Leanne and Mandy. All the birth and marriage dates are listed to the best of my knowledge. Let me add you and Noah now with the kids."

As Ellen listed the names and dates of the births and marriage of her little family, Mr. Engle wrote them in pen on the chart. With sparkling eyes, Ellen watched the simple yet poignant action overcome with the powerful imagery of roots once again. Her little branch was now securely connected to a tree of the generations! The significance made her giddy.

Interrupting her swirling thoughts, Mr. Engle added, "Sometimes it's hard to get information, and Jo has not been in touch with the family in a long time. There is another relative, Yitzi Engle, who lives in Israel who also keeps a list. I will contact him to see if he has any new updates on your branch of the tree."

"That would be wonderful. Thanks – thanks for everything," Ellen said bringing herself back to the conversation.

The Engles had graciously dug up assorted family photos to show to Ellen and Noah. For the next half an hour the little group squeezed together on the multicolored La-Z-boy sofa as Ellen was introduced and Noah often re-introduced to more of the relations.

Chapter Twenty-Nine

November 18, 2007

"NO WAY!" the crowd roared as the Ravens players made their way back out onto the field. The football game between the Baltimore Ravens and the Cleveland Browns was sent into overtime after a field goal kick by the Browns was reviewed, overruled and determined fair. Noah and Ellen had already left their seats when the new ruling came in. They heard it on the televised screens by the concession stands as they made their way to the exit. Noah pulled Ellen back in to the first section they reached.

"Let's watch overtime from here for a while," he said close to her ear as they reached a crowded railing that faced the field. Everyone was on their feet screaming – the whole stadium was in an uproar. Ellen shook her head.

She had been weary with relief as the game had "ended", but this was getting to be a bit much. Usually she enjoyed going to the games, she understood the game well and had become a true fan over the past few years. She and Noah attended most of the home games each season and except for the cold, Ellen truly enjoyed herself. But not today! Today was too much. She had wanted to beg off, and she was not exactly sure why she had not. Throughout the whole tense game she had been planning and strategizing what she would say to her biological mother if she found her, which suddenly seemed both very likely and an exhilarating, terrifying thought.

Although the Ravens had the first possession in the overtime, it was the Browns who were able to capitalize on theirs, getting rapidly into field goal range and scoring the winning field goal just six minutes into the overtime quarter. "Unbelievably disappointing! This is one for the history books. That kick in the fourth quarter will be all over the news tonight," Noah said as he took Ellen's gloved hand in his, and they made their way for the second time to the exit.

Ellen was disappointed in the outcome but exceedingly glad it was over. They trudged through the crowd and made their way to the car parked a good fifteen minute walk away. "Why don't we just heat up the leftovers from Sabbath for dinner?" Ellen ventured. "The game took a long time and I don't feel much like making anything." The truth was that Ellen hated cooking and wasn't very sure she could concentrate on putting anything together.

"That's fine. Do we have some of the roast from Friday night?"

"Sure. I think we have plenty."

After dinner, the quick reheat in the microwave, Noah settled in to watch the nighttime football game, and Ellen went upstairs to their bedroom. She sat on the edge of the bed and dug through her pocketbook, pulled out the folded paper Milton Engle had given her the night before and flattened the page on her bedside table. She found the number for Mandy Romano on the paper and carefully picked up the phone on the bedside table. If she picks up, what will I actually say? Ellen wondered briefly, dialing. With each number her heart pumped furiously.

"Hello," a woman's voice answered on the line.

"Hello, I…," Ellen said tentatively, "am doing a study, and I was directed to you? Are you Mandy Romano?"

"Yes, what do you want?"

"I'm doing a study and I am trying to find Jo Engle." Ellen repeated the lame story trying not to scare Mandy.

"Who are you?" Mandy demanded in a stronger voice.

"I am not so good at this it seems," Ellen admitted, "I am not doing a study, but I didn't want to frighten you. My name is Ellen Sachs and I am adopted." Ellen continued with determination. "I just found out on Friday that my biological mother is Jo Engle. Please don't be upset with me for calling this way, but I am may be your half-sister." Ellen breathed deeply waiting for any response, holding her breath and sincerely hoping that the phone would not be slammed down in her ear. What a botched job she was doing? With all the stewing all day, couldn't she have done better than this?

"I knew about you," Mandy replied matter-of-factly.

"You did. Really? That's amazing. I didn't know about you until last night when Jo's cousin gave me your phone number."

"How did he know how to find me?"

"He keeps a genealogy chart of the family and he had you listed with your sister Leanne. He looked you both up on the web and found your number, but he wasn't able to find Leanne. How long did you know about me?" Ellen asked stunned by how surreal the conversation was getting.

"I've known about you since I was a teenager. Mom was at the doctor and he asked how many pregnancies she had. When she answered three, I reminded her that there were only two of us, and she told me that there was another. She told me she had given her first born up for adoption. I guess that would be you."

"Wow that must have been weird for you. That's incredible." Plowing ahead resolutely, Ellen continued, "Speaking of your mother, I would truly like to talk to her if she would be willing. Would you feel comfortable giving me her phone number?" Mandy hesitated and Ellen waited a few moments then added quickly, "If you don't think she would want me to call her, maybe you could give her my number."

"Tell me your number and I'll see what I can do. What's your name again?"

Thinking that her half-sister sounded like a lawyer by her confident answers and the way she was able to non-commit anything about Jo without sounding hostile, Ellen listed her name and her number. "Mandy, I know this is a difficult situation. If your mother does not want anything to do with me, I will really understand, but could you please give her a message for me either way?" Gathering herself Ellen said, "Please tell her that she did the right thing and that I had a good life. I know that this is what I would want to know and if nothing else I would like to share that with her."

"Ok, Ellen. I'll call you back."

"Thank you Mandy." They hung up and Ellen thought, Well that is that. I'll never hear back from her that's for sure. She went downstairs to tell Noah.

"Noah, it was crazy talking to Mandy. She knew about me and I didn't even think of the possibility of her. She was so controlled through the conversation and I was a mess, and I was the one who called her!"

"Let me get this straight, Ellen. You just cold-called your half-sister? Just like that."

"I know. I'm a lunatic! I have to find Jo. I have to get solid proof for Rabbi Golden."

"Did she tell you anything about your mother?"

"No, not about her now, but she did say that her mother had told her that she had a third pregnancy and that she put her first born up for adoption. That pretty much confirms all of this. WOW, Noah. Can you believe this?"

"Things are moving very fast," he replied. "Are you ready for any of this?"

"No. Not really. But I have to keep going while things are happening."

Not a half hour had gone by when the phone rang. Ellen glanced over at Noah and then picked up the phone from the table.

"Hello," an unknown female voice said, "My name is Leanne. My sister Mandy just called me." Ellen waved the phone at Noah and mouthed excitedly, "the other half-sister!"

"Yes. Hello. So amazing to hear from you!"

"I am amazed too. I didn't know about you until Mandy just told me."

"Really? Mandy seems to have known about me for a while."

"I know. Strange that no one mentioned it to me. Anyway, Mandy and I were wondering if you would be okay with a conference call. We both want to speak to you."

"Sure. Of course," Ellen said as she walked back up to the bedroom. She needed a quiet area to concentrate.

"Great. Hold on a minute while I connect with Mandy."

"Okay."

This is surreal, Ellen thought. A few moments later, Mandy and Leanne were on the line. "Well, hello there both of you," Ellen said.

"We wanted to speak to you together, "Leanne began, "because we needed to tell you something important." Pausing for a heartbeat she continued, "We are sorry to tell you that our mother died almost a year ago. In a week, it will be exactly one year."

"I'm so sorry to hear that," Ellen said with a jolt. Tamping down the emotional response elicited by the hearing of this seminal news, Ellen maintained course. "Was she ill?"

"No. Not really. She had high blood pressure and stopped taking her medication. She died of an aneurism," Leanne replied.

"Oh. I'm so sorry. It sounds like her death was unexpected. That must be hard for both of you."

"Yes, it was," Leanne said. "Her husband sent us her ashes and we spread them at a church in our area. A very peaceful place. If you want, we can take you there."

"At a church? Why a church? I don't understand. Wasn't Jo Jewish?" Ellen asked thoroughly confused. Things were getting rather strange.

"No, she wasn't Jewish. She converted to Christianity a few years ago," Leanne stated cheerfully. "I also converted a short time before her."

"I haven't converted yet, but I am getting close," Mandy added.

"I think I see," Ellen said although she didn't really get it. According to what she had been taught, Jewish people are still considered Jewish even if they convert. It is not something that can be given up. It is something you are born to or possibly convert into. More viscerally disturbing to her was the idea of cremation. A few years back, she and Noah had gone on a synagogue mission to Poland. They had walked the walk of the Holocaust victims at Auschwitz, and they had traveled by night to Majdanek and seen the crematoriums by flashlight. The image of the enormous Plexiglas enclosed mound of human remain ashes at Majdanek, attesting to the brutal slaughter of many thousands of innocent Jewish people by cremation, was all that Ellen could picture. The horrific idea of her own biological mother being cremated, a totally non-Jewish concept, unmanned her. She thought about the Zaka workers in Israel and how they worked methodically and painstakingly to gather every bit of human remains to bury with the dead when suicide bombers succeeded in blowing up innocent victims. The body must be kept intact. Of course, Ellen knew that cremation was an option for the world at large, she worked in the Vital Events office where cremation was a choice on the death certificate information that was gathered. The thoughts ran quickly through her mind, each vying for

215

attention, but Ellen knew the thoughts would be there later and she forced her attention back to the present. Her two half-sisters waited for her answer.

"I don't think I want to do that just yet," she managed to answer. "Maybe you can give me the address and we can talk about it later. Everything is happening rather fast."

"No problem," Leanne said.

"Would you tell me a bit about Jo? You said her husband – did you mean your father?"

"No, our parents divorced when we were young. Our mother's second husband died and she married a third. That's the one that sent the ashes to us."

The revelations came fast and quick for the next hour. With surprising ease the three women shared information about their husbands and children, careers and lives. Ellen frantically wrote notes trying to piece together disjointed information into something she could work later to understand. Her half-sisters threw in tidbits about their mother and Ellen was intrigued, something she hadn't expected. As the hour grew late, Leanne asked, "Do you want to get together and see some pictures?"

"Yes. I really would," Ellen replied surprising herself.

"Maybe you could bring some pictures of your family too," Leanne added.

"That's a good idea. I'll bring along some pictures of the cousins that helped me find you as well." Ellen said enthusiastically, failing to notice the lack of response to this idea across the phone lines. "What day do you want to meet?"

The following Wednesday at lunchtime was agreed upon by all. Oh my goodness! What a day, thought Ellen, as she hung up the phone. Staring at her disjointed notes, she felt a strange connection to the poem by Robert Frost, "The Road Not Taken", in which he most eloquently wrote, "Two roads diverged in a yellow wood, And sorry I could not travel both." From the moment of her conception she had traveled a certain road and path, and in her mind's eye she could see how two paths met and shortly after her birth, by the adoption, she was set on a completely different path. The reality was that her life would have been utterly unlike the one she had known. At the crossroads, her mother by birth, Jo, had stood and looked down both roads as far as she could see. She had made the pivotal decision that set Ellen on the other road, the road away from her, the one less traveled, that of an adoptee. Robert Frost continued in the poem with the stirring words, "Yet knowing how way leads on to way, I doubted if I should ever come back." In a way, Ellen felt she was finding her way back, finding the clues and glimpsing the emerging image of the first road, the road not taken.

Quickly, she filled Noah in on the extraordinary conversation and then prepared for bed. Emotional and physical exhaustion prevailed as Ellen fell into a deep slumber.

Chapter Thirty

November 21, 2007

Ellen plugged the IHOP address into her GPS. Jo's three daughters had chosen a location for their first meeting approximately a 30-minute drive for each of them. The ironic fact that they lived in a one-hour radius from each other was not lost on the trio.

"I have always had a strong gut feeling that my family was right here all along," Ellen had reiterated to Noah earlier that day.

"I know you have, honey. You have told me that through the years. It's wild that you were actually right," Noah had responded before heading to work.

As Ellen thought back on the brief conversation and the fact that she was truly not surprised to realize she was correct, she adjusted her orange cap and smoothed out her blunt cut chin-length hair. For religious reasons, she always wore a head covering when out of the home and had taken on that particular Orthodox Jewish custom years before. She had chosen her outfit carefully, a flattering black skirt and comfortable long sleeve black tee with an orange sweatshirt that matched her cap and was bought for just that reason. Dressed in one of her favorite outfits of the season, Ellen felt a bit better, the familiarity of her comfy well-worn clothes helped to lessen some of her anxiety. Will I look like them?

Ellen ruminated as she pulled on her favorite black boots.

Following the GPS commands, Ellen found her way easily. The lively beat of "Life is a Highway" coming from her car radio mixed with the rapid beat of her heart as she reached her destination. Turning into the parking lot, she looked around intently noticing each car and any occupants. As she pulled in, she saw a woman about her own age with short dark wavy hair, slightly taller than Ellen but also on the petite side, emerge from a car three spaces over. The woman waited by her car as Ellen parked. Ellen got out of her car and leaned back in to grab her glasses which were propped up in the cup holder. Straightening, she was momentarily startled when the woman suddenly appeared close behind her.

"Are you Ellen?" the woman asked as she studied Ellen's face.

"Yes, I am. Are you Leanne or Mandy?" Ellen responded excitedly.

"Leanne," she said leaning in for a tentative hug.

Ellen hugged her and then pulled back holding her at arm's length to take a good look. "It's so nice to meet you."

"You too," Leanne said looking Ellen up and down. "I don't think we look much alike at all."

"No. I agree with you," Ellen laughed as her own thought was voiced. "Although we do both have brown hair and we are almost the same size," Ellen said with encouragement. Leanne stood only an inch or so taller than Ellen and dressed in jeans and a beige cable knit sweater with a blue turtleneck, she looked earthy and relaxed. "Is Mandy here yet?"

"She's probably waiting inside. I thought I saw her car over by the door," Leanne responded. "Let's go find her."

Together the two walked the short distance to the front of the building and inside sneaking peeks at each other along the way. They quickly found Mandy standing in the entranceway rifling through a small photo album.

"Hi Mandy," Leanne said smiling as she and Ellen approached. "Look who I found outside. Ellen, this is Mandy."

"Hi Mandy. It's great to meet you," Ellen said noticing that Mandy's softer features were a closer match to her own yet no real resemblance. Her hair was also dark brown but a more golden brown worn shoulder length with deep waves. She stood at least five inches taller than Ellen wearing flats, and her appearance suggested professional in a white blouse and charcoal gray slacks.

"Hi Ellen. I'm glad to meet you too," she responded.

"Let's move inside and get a seat," Leanne prompted moving the small group forward through the inner doors.

"We would like seating for three," Leanne answered the hostess.

Once seated at a small rectangular table, Mandy and Leanne pointed at a table two over from theirs. "Some of our father's relatives are here this morning as well. We'll just say hi and be right back," Leanne said as she and Mandy moved off.

Ellen adjusted herself and then watched as they said their hellos to their father's relatives. I wonder if anyone knows who my father is, Ellen thought. I wonder if their father knows.

Within moments, Leanne and Mandy were back at the table and as they settled in Leanne began, "Let's order first and then look through the pictures. I brought a bunch and Mandy has a small album and it looks like you brought some things as well Ellen."

"I did. I gathered pictures of my husband and kids and of me at different stages of my life. Plus I brought pictures of the Engle family – the ones we have been friendly with through the years." Ellen noticed a quick pointed look pass between her two half-sisters at the mention of the Engles. She decided not to question them about the significance at that point, but tucked the query in her mind for future reference.

Once they had ordered and Ellen had explained about her observance of the laws of keeping kosher, she sipped on a glass of water while the sisters ate. Within minutes pictures were strewn across the table.

"Here are some that I found of our mother," Leanne said passing a small pile of individual photos across the table to Ellen.

Carefully Ellen inspected the photos of their mother all but one of which was taken of her as a very young child. Ellen noted that her own childhood pictures did share a bit of a resemblance, enhanced by the fact that both she and her mother sported identical haircuts, short wavy dark hair with straight bangs. The square jaw facial shape was also a match.

"Is this your grandmother Louisa with her in these two pictures?" Ellen asked holding up a large formal looking photo of Jo on a woman's lap in an attractive oversized chair with a portly gentleman standing beside them and a small wallet sized photograph of a strikingly beautiful woman holding a toddler. It was hard to determine if the woman in the two photographs was the same person, her appearance had changed radically her face and body much fuller and bloated in the latter picture. Also in the second photo, both the child and woman were smiling and seemed happy while in the first their expressions were somewhat pained.

"Yes, that is our grandmother Louisa and our grandfather William in the one picture," Leanne said.

"She had cancer, didn't she?" Ellen asked.

"Yes. I think so." Mandy answered. "She died way before we were born."

"I guess that may explain why she looks so different in the two pictures. They must have been taken about four years apart, and according to what I have been told, she was sick for all or most of those four years." Unsure, the sisters just shrugged.

Picking up the only picture from the pile on the table of Jo in which she was moderately older probably teenage or young twenties, Ellen commented, "She was a very pretty young woman."

"I think you look more like her than we do. What do you think Mandy?" Leanne asked.

"Maybe. Yes. I see what you mean," Mandy concurred. "I think that's a picture of Mom when she was a camp counselor."

"Do you know what camp?" Ellen asked noting the open, relaxed expression and warm smile on her mother's face. She looked happy and content.

"No," Leanne voiced as Mandy shook her head.

"Do you have any recent photos?" Ellen continued.

"I have one – this one of our mother taken shortly before she died. She was living in Arizona at that time," Mandy offered.

Ellen looked closely at the picture of a much older, heavier Jo in a loose-flowing dress. She still had the same open smile but her eyes looked wistful as though life's lessons had been learned through hardship and she had seen a great deal.

Having exhausted the small stash of pictures of Jo, Ellen, Leanne and Mandy spent the remainder of their two hours together sharing pictures of their families. Leanne and Mandy took turns showing Ellen pictures of their families identifying their children through all stages, themselves at pivotal times of life, their husbands and finally group photos with both families sharing Thanksgiving and Christmas. Perplexed, Ellen noticed that Jo was not present in any of the family pictures.

"Our parents got divorced when I was eight," Leanne explained. "Our mother did not raise us. We did see her, but we didn't spend a great deal of time together."

"I see," Ellen murmured, yet she didn't really understand. Women of that era were almost always given custody of their children when couples divorced, Ellen reflected. She remembered the 1979 Academy award winning movie, *Kramer vs. Kramer*, in which a divorce and custody battle depicted changing roles of motherhood and fatherhood and a slow moving shift in custody proceedings. Even though the mother in the movie did win custody of the couple's son, the movie brought to light the fact that fathers could also be primary caregivers. Almost two decades prior, conventional wisdom clearly maintained that the mother should be given custody except in very extreme cases. As far as Jo was concerned, subsequent conversations would be needed to get the full, sad truth. The pretty young girl with the open smile gave birth to three daughters, but she didn't raise or nurture any of them.

Ellen shared her large pile of pictures. As she pointed out all the Engle relatives and their children in pictures with her own children, she could see Leanne and Mandy were not overly interested. Ceasing, she finally asked, "Did you know any of the Engle family?"

"A long time ago. Our mother didn't have much to do with any of them. We thought there was some bad blood between them, and so we never really knew the family," Leanne stated.

"That's really unfortunate. All the family members I know are wonderful people. Maybe it's a different generation," Ellen said.

They cleaned up the pictures and prepared to leave. Leanne and Ellen said goodbye to Mandy at the front door.

"It really has been wonderful to meet you," Ellen began. "Maybe we can keep in touch a bit?"

"Sure. You have my number and I have yours," Mandy said.

Leanne and Ellen walked to the back and Ellen paused at Leanne's car. "I'm really glad you found us," Leanne said, hugging Ellen. "Hey, what size shoe do you wear?"

"Eight," Ellen responded with a smile. "What about you?"

"I wear a seven," Leanne answered. "I wonder what else we have in common.

"Do you have bunions?" Ellen asked. "I have had them all my life."

"No. But I do have lots of allergies."

"Well, I have allergies also, but thankfully they are very mild."

"Oh. That's good for you. Let's think about other things and get together again soon," Leanne said.

"Great. Let's talk next week," Ellen suggested.

"Do you think your family would like to meet mine?" Leanne asked.

"I don't know," Ellen replied, "I think Jill might be on board, but to be honest, I think Noah may need a while. He's very supportive, but seems a bit apprehensive at the same time. Why don't you ask your husband and kids and see how they feel and I'll check as well?"

"Okay. We don't really need to rush into anything."

"That's true. Now that we know each other, we have lots of time. Take care, Leanne."

Driving home, Ellen reviewed the encounter. She rolled it in her mind frame by frame like in a movie. The whole situation was profoundly surreal. She had actually found her mother's family. Suddenly, she wanted to find her father's family as well. Her mind in overdrive, she was deep into planning what to do and who to talk to next, when she reigned herself in. I have to keep my eye on the ball, she thought. I still don't have Rabbi Golden's okay.

Shortly after arriving home, Ellen called the good rabbi.

"Rabbi Golden," Ellen began luckily catching him by phone between appointments, "I have unbelievable news! I was able to finagle a copy of my real, actual birth certificate and I found my biological mother's family."

"That's spectacular news," Rabbi Golden responded. "Did you find your mother?"

"Unfortunately she died almost a year ago. Come to think of it, it will be exactly a year this Sunday."

"I'm so sorry, Ellen. Had you felt that you might want to meet her?"

"To be honest, rabbi, I am a bit relieved at this point. I don't think I was ready to meet her."

"That's understandable."

"Yes." Pausing a moment, Ellen continued. "Anyway, the second part of the truly amazing news is that I am part of the Engle family. My mother's name was Jo Engle and she was a first cousin to Milton Engle – which makes me a second cousin to Stan and Rebecca and Meyer and Eve."

"How remarkable!"

"I know. I also found two half-sisters. Milton Engle helped me find them. It has truly been a whirlwind week."

"How are you doing with all the new information?"

"I am starting to process, but to be honest, very overwhelmed. I don't have much time for that yet, so I will get to the point of my call today. Is what I have told you enough to prove my Jewish identity?" Ellen asked holding her breath.

"Hmmm. Since I'm not able to speak directly to your mother, I could speak to Milton Engle. Did he know your mother personally?"

"Yes. He was her first cousin and he knew her growing up."

"Good. I'll speak to him for you, but we need to definitely make sure your grandmother was Jewish as well."

"She passed away many years ago – back in the 1940's. Could Mr. Engle vouch for both my mother and grandmother? He also knew my grandmother."

"I'm not sure. Do you think you could find out where your grandmother was buried? By Jewish law, if she was buried in a Jewish cemetery, we could consider that sufficient proof that she was also Jewish."

"Okay," Ellen said wheels turning, "I know that she was living in Baltimore when she died. I'll try checking with Rosensteins, the Jewish funeral home that has been around for decades, and see if they have the location of her burial plot. Rabbi, let me recap. If I find the burial plot of my grandmother and it's in a Jewish cemetery that will be proof of one generation of Jewish heritage. Then, if we directly ask Mr. Engle, a close relative of my mother, and he vouches for her Jewish heritage, I'll have the two generations that I need to definitively state that I am a Jew."

"I believe so."

"Great. I think this is doable," Ellen said revved up. "Should I just tell Rachel or do we need something more formal for her to take to the rabbi that will be marrying them when the time comes?"

"I think it would be best for me to write you a letter on synagogue letterhead stating your Jewish identity. This way you will have it for any future considerations."

"Great idea. Thank you rabbi. I will get on the grandmother part right away."

"And I'll contact Milton Engle. Excellent detective work, Ellen! I'm so happy for all of you."

"Thank you Rabbi Golden. You are the best!" Sobering, Ellen hesitated and then asked, "Do I have any responsibility as far as mourning and shiva now that I have knowledge my birth mother has died?"

Just a few years prior, Noah's father had been informed that his long lost brother had died. It had taken months after the passing for the news via a lawyer settling the deceased's affairs to reach Ellen's father-in-law. As soon as the news was delivered, Rabbi Golden had informed Noah's father that he needed to begin the Jewish mourning custom of shiva promptly and for the full seven days by Orthodox custom.

"I know you said it will be a year since your birth mother's death, but has it been more than a year by the Hebrew calendar since her passing?" Rabbi Golden asked.

"Just barely. I found out from my half-sisters on the 10th of Kislev (Hebrew month) this year and she died on the 4th of Kislev last year."

"Based on that, my answer is two-fold. Firstly, you do not need to sit shiva, because the year mark passed even if just by a few days. Secondly, as an adopted child you don't have an obligation in our mourning practices for your biological mother. She relinquished you of that obligation when she put you up for adoption."

"Really? No obligation. I'm surprised, because when my mother, I mean my adopted mother Sandra died, Rabbi Berg told me that I didn't have a true obligation to follow the mourning practices for her either. He told me that I had total leeway and could choose what felt right for me. Consequently, I chose to observe the full seven days of shiva even though my brother and step-father sat only three according to their Reform observance, but I did use some latitude throughout the year and was lenient. It's odd that I have no real responsibility toward either mother by Jewish law."

"Yes. It does seem odd, but in this case, halachically (Jewish law) you are free of duty."

The day was fast fading, so Ellen hung up with Rabbi Golden and immediately looked up the number for the primary Jewish funeral home in the area.

"I am trying to find the location of my grandmother's funeral plot. She died in 1949, but I believe your funeral home would surely have handled the funeral," Ellen said.

"Let me look it up for you. What was the name and date of death?"

"Louisa Engle. She died on April 27, 1949."

Ellen waited expectantly as the helpful gentleman looked it up on his computer. "I have the information," he said a few minutes later. "She was buried at the Beth Yehuda Cemetary on April 27, 1949 at 11:40am. Rabbi Emmanuel Goldstein performed the service."

"Fantastic. I didn't know you would have everything so quickly for me."

"Computerized. Glad to help. The Beth Yehuda cemetery is located at 6700 Brown Lane. It's a very old cemetery and there is no caretaker on the premises. Four different synagogues have space there, so it may take a while to find the exact grave. Be careful and take someone with you."

"Thank you very much. I really appreciate your help and advice. It means so much to me," Ellen replied with heartfelt gratitude.

Coincidentally, Rachel was due to come to Baltimore by Greyhound bus that Friday. When Ellen looked up the address for the cemetery, she found that it was just minutes from the Greyhound station. Perfect, Ellen thought, I'll stop with Rachel on our way back. Checking the route, Ellen found a problem. It was much easier to stop on her way to Rachel, the cemetery was just off the highway exit. But the case was not the same for the return route. For some reason there was no exit from that side. Taking the gamble, Ellen stopped on her way to pick up Rachel.

"Noah, I'm calling from the cemetery and I'm by myself. It really is a creepy area. I know you're working, but please keep the phone by you while I search for the grave. I'll scream if something happens and you can call 911."

"Ellen, this isn't the greatest plan," Noah complained.

"I know. I know. Just hang in there for me. I'll be quick."

Determined, Ellen darted up and down all the rows. Some gravestones were hard to read and the alignment was difficult. Frustrated and nerve racked, she spoke into the phone every few minutes, so Noah knew she was okay. A half hour later, she still couldn't locate her grandmother's plot.

"Noah, this is impossible. I know it must be here, but I'm getting more and more agitated."

"Give it up, Ellen. I'll go back with you next week."

"Okay. You're right. This was stupid."

"Good. Tell me when you're safely back in the car."

After about a minute, Ellen replied, "I'm there. I'm on my way to pick up Rachel." Dejected, Ellen clicked the door lock and pulled her camera from her shoulder bag dumping it on the seat next to her. So much for a picture of the gravestone, she thought.

The next day, on the Sabbath, Ellen was in synagogue when Rabbi Golden spotted her. "Ellen, did you find your grandmother's grave?"

"Oh rabbi, I went to the cemetery and let me tell you it was very creepy. There is no caretaker, and therefore no one to direct me. I looked and looked but I didn't find the grave."

"I'm sorry."

"It wasn't fun. Noah said he'll go with me next week. I did find out that Rabbi Emmanuel Goldstein presided at the funeral. We are friends with his son, so that was cool."

"Rabbi Emmanuel Goldstein is a very prominent rabbi in Baltimore."

"Yes, I know."

"Ellen, if he did the service that would be proof enough that your grandmother was Jewish."

"Rabbi, are you saying that I don't need a picture of the grave?"

"That's exactly what I'm saying. Ellen, you've done it! I spoke with Mr. Engle yesterday and I feel very comfortable writing the letter for you with the information you have uncovered."

"YES!" Ellen exclaimed pumping her fists into the air reminiscent of Rocky Balboa when he won the heavyweight championship against Apollo Creed. Rabbi Golden laughed along with Ellen, and they both beamed.

Chapter Thirty-One

January 2008

Rachel and Daniel's engagement became official with whoops and cheers and mazal tovs. The wedding day was fast approaching.

"Noah, I decided to go to New York tomorrow and spend the day with Rachel," Ellen said. "We need a fun girlie day before the wedding."

"Great idea. Do you need me to take or pick you up from the station?"

"No thanks. I'm taking the Riley Bus from the mall, and I'll be able to leave my car there for the day. The bus gets back 9:30 or so. Do you want me to pick you up a deli sandwich from the city?"

"Sure. That would be great. Corned beef and pastrami with Russian dressing sounds perfect. Thanks. And bring me back a kiss from Rachel too."

"I will."

At work the following Monday, "Kelly," Ellen began somewhat tentatively, "I've been wondering."

"Go ahead Ellen, whatever it is," Kelly prompted with a pretty good idea of the nature of Ellen's quandary.

"How come you were able to look up my information and give me my birth certificate? It seems to me that the commitment to maintain the privacy of the sealed record was between the state and the birth mother. I didn't know anything at all about my birth mother."

"I thought you might figure that out. To be honest, I did some checking to see if I could help you. I looked up your birth certificate, and then I checked for death records. You're right. I didn't have the right to share the information with you until I realized that your biological mother was deceased. The fact that your adopted parents were gone and the fact you are the remaining member of the adoption triad allowed me to give you the information. I'm so sorry to hear about your mother, but I'm glad that you found some family."

"I just knew something was funny. Thanks. Thanks for that and thanks for sharing. Finally it makes sense to me. I really appreciate your help and candor, Kelly," Ellen said smiling. "And your friendship," she continued as she gave Kelly a hug.

At lunchtime the same day, Ellen closed her office door, sat down heavily in her chair behind her outdated but functional desk and picked up the phone. She had been putting off this call. She took a few calming breaths as she punched in the numbers, hoping to slow her racing heart.

"Michael," she said. "I have news. Where are you?"

"I'm in Florida. I just finished a round."

"Great. How did you do?" Ellen asked as she pictured Michael in shorts and a bright colored tee shirt sitting in his sporty red convertible, roof down, soaking up the sun. She, on the other hand, was dressed in a gray turtleneck with a black cardigan suitable for the dreary winter weather in Baltimore, huddled behind her desk in a windowless office.

"The course beat me again."

"That's too bad. It's only mini-golf for me. Anyway, do you have a minute?"

"Just a few. I am meeting the guys for lunch."

Ploughing ahead quickly, Ellen said, "I have been researching my biological family. I know this is a bit out of the blue, but it became important to prove my Jewish identity."

"Did you find out anything?"

"Yes. I actually did. I found out who my birth mother was – she died over a year ago – and I found a whole bunch of cousins and two half-sisters."

"Wow! Incredible!" He exclaimed. "How did you do that?"

"It's a long story. I'll tell you one day when you have more time."

"I'm really happy for you," he said. Ellen heard the catch in his throat. "I always wondered if you would search for them," he said after a long moment. His obvious emotional response brought tears to Ellen's eyes.

"I wasn't sure how you would feel about this," Ellen said, brushing away a stray tear from her right eye with the back of her forefinger. She was pleasantly touched and relieved by Michael's response.

"I think it's great. I really do. You said your mother died….," he trailed off.

"She did. About a year ago. I wasn't sure I was ready to meet her, but it is sad."

"I'm sorry. Did you also say sisters?"

"Yes. I met them and they are nice, but they had a hard time growing up. I have no idea where any of this will go," she thought out loud. "One thing I do know for certain is that I was the lucky one. Mom and Dad gave me a better life."

"They did a good job," he said succinctly. "I really have to go. I'm glad you found them. I can't wait to tell Diana. We will see you at the wedding."

"Yes. The big day is coming."

***

"Noah," Ellen said, looking up from her romance novel as the two sat reading side by side on the living room sofa. "I had a disturbing thought."

"What's up, buttercup?" he asked, pulling himself away from the interesting article he was reading in Sports Illustrated.

"Stan and Meyer are almost the same age that I am. I could have married one of them."

"And here I thought I was the special one," he replied, making a mock pouty face.

"Of course, you're the only one I ever wanted to marry," she insisted quickly with a grin. "I'm just saying that it was possible. We are of an age, and we were living in close proximity. Our paths could have crossed, and we could have dated. It isn't inconceivable, and yet we are cousins, second cousins, close relatives."

"That's true. It was all possible."

"But that's terrible. Think about it. What would've happened if we had found out that we were cousins?"

"I don't know, but I'm truly glad we aren't. That's for sure."

"Thank goodness, we didn't end up relatives! With all that I've learned in the past few months about my adoption, I'm even more convinced that adoptees need to know their heritage. It really is irresponsible to keep the information from them. I'm angry that I had to go dig it up, yet I realize how lucky I am. I was able to find what I needed to find. All adoptees simply need to know!"

"I agree 100 percent. But you know what? I'm feeling lucky too," he said, pulling her close for a kiss.

Chapter Thirty-Two

July 2008

Ellen, in a floor length wine-colored ball gown, and Noah dressed in a finely-cut black suit, flanked Rachel, each holding onto one of her arms, as they walked toward the chupah (Jewish marriage canopy). Rachel looked radiant in her elegant soft-white wedding dress and flowing train. As they made their way, Ellen looked around at the smiling faces of their family and friends with great joy. Her gaze immediately found Michael, fit and trim, his height making him easy to spot. Passing Melinda, Eve and Michelle on her left and Stan and Meyer on the right, Ellen made purposeful eye contact with each of them. A few steps later, she smiled at Leanne and Mandy grateful that the two new additions to her life had made the effort to share in the special day. Joined by Rachel's soon to be mother-in-law, Ellen walked Rachel around her groom the requisite seven times and then finally took her place next to Noah. She reached for his hand, and the two stood united watching as their eldest daughter was transformed from a bride into a married woman, a Jewish married woman, with no question of her heritage and no encumbrances on her status. The glass was broken, the service completed and shouts of mazal tov (best wishes) filled the air. Ellen found her eyes damp with happiness as she and Rachel embraced.

Much later, when the catering crew was cleaning up and all the guests had gone, Rachel exclaimed, "Thank you so much for everything Mom!"

Daniel, her new son-in-law and as her dear friend Wendy often said son-in-love, continued the thought, "It was a perfect wedding, Mom!"

Crushing them both in a big hug, Ellen replied, "You are both very welcome. I'm so glad everything worked out beautifully."

Ellen was deeply relieved that "everything" had worked out. Her planning for the wedding had been filled with an additional task, a true labor of love making sure that the young couple's path was clear, her daughters' identities and that of their descendants unquestioned by Jewish law. Thoroughly touched, Ellen felt that she was truly one of the lucky ones. She had been able to overcome the obstacles and find a way to disclose the information so closely guarded by the system. A confluence of circumstances had certainly presented themselves to aid in her efforts. Perhaps it had been destined that she never meet her mother, and therefore her birth mother had died when she did, so the search would be successful. Perhaps, she had been destined to work in Vital Events rather than any other state position in the area, because that is how she was meant to find the information she sought. Perhaps the answer was that she had persevered when others would have chosen a less challenging path. No matter, she thought, buoyed by the success. As she looked upon the glowing faces of her children, she determined that it had all been worth it. Everything in her life had led to this one perfect moment, this one perfect beginning.

Thank you for reading my book. I hope my story touched you. If you enjoyed it, won't you please take a moment to leave me a review at your favorite retailer.

My sincerest appreciation,
Judy Pachino